KU-278-082

CGP has National 5 Maths covered!

There's a lot to learn for the SQA National 5 Maths exams, but never fear — this brilliant CGP Revision Guide explains it all as clearly and simply as possible.

We've also added a helping of exam-style questions to test you on what you've learned, plus a few daft jokes to keep you motivated. There's no better way to revise!

How to access your free Online Edition

This book includes a free Online Edition to read on your PC, Mac or tablet. To access it, just go to **cgpbooks.co.uk/extras** and enter this code...

2451 9694 1905 6754

By the way, this code only works for one person. If somebody else has used this book before you, they might have already claimed the Online Edition.

CGP — the best by miles! ☺

Our sole aim here at CGP is to produce the highest quality books — carefully written, immaculately presented and dangerously close to being funny.

Then we work our socks off to get them out to you — at the cheapest possible prices.

Published by CGP

Written by Richard Parsons

Editors:
Tom Miles, Alison Palin, Caley Simpson

With thanks to Ian MacAndie and Dave Ryan for the proofreading.

ISBN: 978 1 78294 943 5

Clipart from Corel®
Printed by Elanders Ltd, Newcastle upon Tyne

Text, design, layout and original illustrations © Coordination Group Publications Ltd. (CGP) 2018
All rights reserved.

Photocopying more than one chapter of this book is not permitted. Extra copies are available from CGP with next day delivery.
0800 1712 712 • www.cgpbooks.co.uk

Contents

Fractions

Here's a nice gentle start to National 5 Maths — fractions. These pages show you how to cope with fraction calculations without your beloved calculator (in case they come up on the non-calculator paper).

Here's a Quick Reminder of Some Key Fraction Skills

1) To cancel down or simplify a fraction, divide top and bottom by the same number, until they won't go further. For example, to simplify $\frac{18}{24}$, divide top and bottom by 6 (the HCF of 18 and 24) to get $\frac{3}{4}$.

2) Mixed numbers are things like $3\frac{1}{3}$, with an integer part and a fraction part.
Improper fractions are ones where the top number is larger than the bottom number.
You need to be able to convert between these two forms:

EXAMPLES:

1. Write $4\frac{2}{3}$ as an improper fraction.

1) Think of the mixed number as an addition:
$$4\frac{2}{3} = 4 + \frac{2}{3}$$

2) Turn the integer part into a fraction:
$$4 + \frac{2}{3} = \frac{12}{3} + \frac{2}{3} = \frac{12+2}{3} = \frac{14}{3}$$

2. Write $\frac{31}{4}$ as a mixed number.

Divide the top number by the bottom.
1) The answer gives the whole number part.
2) The remainder goes on top of the fraction.
$$31 \div 4 = 7 \text{ remainder } 3 \text{ so } \frac{31}{4} = 7\frac{3}{4}$$

3) To find a fraction of something, multiply the fraction by the number — so to find $\frac{9}{20}$ of £360, you do $\frac{9}{20} \times £360 = (£360 \div 20) \times 9 = £18 \times 9 = £162$. You could have multiplied £360 by the numerator (9) before dividing by the denominator (20) here — whichever you find easier.

4) To write one number as a fraction of another, just write the first number as the numerator and the second as the denominator and cancel down — for example, 180 as a fraction of 80 is $\frac{180}{80} = \frac{9}{4}$.

Multiply Numerators and Denominators Separately

To multiply two fractions, just multiply top and bottom separately.
It usually helps to cancel down first if you can.

EXAMPLE: Evaluate $\frac{8}{15} \times \frac{5}{12}$.

8 and 12 both divide by 4

Cancel down by dividing top and bottom by any common factors you find in either fraction:

$$\frac{{}^{2}\cancel{8}}{15} \times \frac{5}{{}_{3}\cancel{12}} = \frac{2}{{}^{1}\cancel{15}_{3}} \times \frac{\cancel{5}}{3}$$

15 and 5 both divide by 5

Now multiply the top and bottom numbers separately:

$$= \frac{2}{3} \times \frac{1}{3} = \frac{2 \times 1}{3 \times 3} = \frac{2}{9}$$

To Divide, Turn the Second Fraction Upside Down

To divide one fraction by another, turn the second fraction UPSIDE DOWN and then multiply:

EXAMPLE: Find $2\frac{1}{3} \div 3\frac{1}{2}$.

Rewrite the mixed numbers as improper fractions:
$$2\frac{1}{3} \div 3\frac{1}{2} = \frac{7}{3} \div \frac{7}{2}$$

Turn $\frac{7}{2}$ upside down and multiply:
$$= \frac{7}{3} \times \frac{2}{7}$$

Simplify by cancelling the 7s:
$$= \frac{1}{3} \times \frac{2}{1} = \frac{2}{3}$$

When you're multiplying or dividing with mixed numbers, always turn them into improper fractions first.

Fractions

You're not quite done with fractions yet — you also need to know how to add and subtract them.

To Add or Subtract, Find a Common Denominator

1) Before you can add or subtract fractions, you need to find a number that all the denominators divide into — this will be your common denominator. The simplest way is to find the lowest common multiple of the denominators.

2) Once you've found a common denominator, rewrite all the fractions with this denominator — then just add or subtract the numerators only.

3) If you're adding or subtracting mixed numbers, it usually helps to convert them to improper fractions first (especially when doing subtractions).

EXAMPLE: Calculate $2\frac{1}{5} - 1\frac{1}{2}$.

Rewrite the mixed numbers as improper fractions: $\quad 2\frac{1}{5} - 1\frac{1}{2} = \frac{11}{5} - \frac{3}{2}$

Find a common denominator: $\quad\quad\quad\quad\quad\quad = \frac{22}{10} - \frac{15}{10}$

Subtract the numerators: $\quad\quad\quad\quad\quad\quad\quad = \frac{22-15}{10} = \frac{7}{10}$

You Might Have to Combine the Operations

In the exam, you might get a question where you need to use a combination of adding, subtracting, multiplying and dividing fractions — it might even include brackets. If you get a question like this, don't panic — just take it one step at a time, and remember the rules of BODMAS:

Brackets, Other, Division, Multiplication, Addition, Subtraction

BODMAS tells you the ORDER in which these operations should be done — work out Brackets first, then Other things like squaring, then Divide and Multiply before Adding and Subtracting. To decide between dividing/multiplying or adding/subtracting, just work from left to right.

EXAMPLE: Evaluate $\frac{3}{5}\left(\frac{1}{6} + \frac{3}{4}\right)$.

Deal with the bit in brackets first — find a common denominator and add the numerators: $\quad \frac{3}{5}\left(\frac{1}{6} + \frac{3}{4}\right) = \frac{3}{5}\left(\frac{2}{12} + \frac{9}{12}\right) = \frac{3}{5}\left(\frac{11}{12}\right)$

Cancel down by dividing the 3 and the 12 by 3: $\quad = \frac{\overset{1}{\cancel{3}}}{5} \times \frac{11}{\underset{4}{\cancel{12}}} = \frac{1}{5} \times \frac{11}{4}$

Multiply the numerators and denominators separately: $\quad = \frac{11}{20}$

No fractions were harmed in the making of these pages...

...although one was slightly frightened for a while, and several were tickled. When you think you've learnt all this, try all of these Exam Practice Questions without a calculator.

Q1 Evaluate: a) $\frac{3}{8} \times 1\frac{5}{12}$ [2 marks]   b) $1\frac{7}{9} \div 2\frac{2}{3}$ [2 marks]

           c) $4\frac{1}{9} + 2\frac{2}{27}$ [2 marks]   d) $9\frac{1}{4} - 5\frac{2}{3}$ [2 marks]

Q2 Evaluate $\left(1\frac{1}{5} - \frac{2}{3}\right) \div \frac{3}{5}$. Give your answer in its simplest form.   [3 marks]

Rounding

When rounding, think about the <u>level of accuracy</u> you need — for example, you'd probably give your height in metres to 2 decimal places, but the distance between cities in miles to the nearest mile.

Make Sure You're Happy Rounding to Decimal Places

Here's a handy method for how to round to a given number of <u>decimal places</u>:

1) <u>IDENTIFY</u> the position of the '<u>LAST DIGIT</u>' from the number of decimal places.
2) Then look at the next digit to the <u>RIGHT</u> — called <u>THE DECIDER</u>.
3) If the <u>DECIDER</u> is <u>5 OR MORE</u>, then <u>ROUND UP</u> the <u>LAST DIGIT</u>.
   If the <u>DECIDER</u> is <u>4 OR LESS</u>, then <u>LEAVE</u> the <u>LAST DIGIT</u> as it is.
4) There must be <u>NO MORE DIGITS</u> after the last digit (not even zeros).

'Last digit' = last one in the <u>rounded</u> version, not the original number.

EXAMPLE: What is 7.45839 to 2 decimal places?

7.45839   =   7.46

LAST DIGIT   DECIDER

The <u>LAST DIGIT</u> rounds <u>UP</u> because the <u>DECIDER</u> is <u>5 or more</u>.

If you have to <u>round up</u> a <u>9</u> (to 10), replace the 9 with 0, and <u>carry 1</u> to the left. Remember to keep enough <u>zeros</u> to fill the right number of decimal places — so to 2 d.p. <u>45.699</u> would be rounded to <u>45.70</u>, and <u>64.996</u> would be rounded to <u>65.00</u>.

65 has the same value as 65.00, but 65 isn't expressed to 2 d.p. so it would be marked wrong.

Rounding to Significant Figures is Similar

The method for significant figures is <u>identical</u> to that for decimal places except that locating the <u>last digit</u> is more difficult — it wouldn't be so bad, but for the <u>zeros</u>...

1) The <u>1st significant figure</u> of any number is simply <u>the first digit which isn't a zero</u>.

2) The <u>2nd, 3rd, 4th, etc. significant figures</u> follow on immediately after the 1st, <u>regardless of being zeros or not zeros</u>.

I asked Stacey for her significant figures.

Data?

Nah, we're just friends.

0.002309   2.03070

SIG. FIGS: 1st 2nd 3rd 4th   1st 2nd 3rd 4th

(If you're rounding to say, 3 s.f., then the LAST DIGIT is simply the 3rd sig. fig.)

3) After <u>rounding</u> the <u>last digit</u>, <u>end zeros</u> must be filled in up to, <u>but not beyond</u>, the decimal point.

No <u>extra zeros</u> must ever be put in <u>after</u> the decimal point.

EXAMPLES:

		to 3 s.f.	to 2 s.f.	to 1 s.f.
1)	54.7651	54.8	55	50
2)	0.0045902	0.00459	0.0046	0.005
3)	30 895.4 km	30 900 km	31 000 km	30 000 km

Be careful — you should only round the <u>answer</u> to a calculation, not during the working. If you round too early, your final answer will be <u>inaccurate</u> or even <u>wrong</u>.

Percentages

You should be pretty familiar with percentages, but I'll go over some of the basics as a quick refresher.

'Per Cent' Means 'Out of 100'

1) To find $\underline{x\% \text{ of } y}$, turn the percentage into a $\underline{\text{decimal/fraction}}$, then $\underline{\text{multiply}}$.
   E.g. 15% of £46 = $\frac{15}{100}$ × £46 = £6.90 (you could have multiplied by 0.15 instead here).

2) To write $\underline{x \text{ as a percentage of } y}$, $\underline{\text{divide}}$ x by y, then multiply by $\underline{100}$.
   E.g. 209 as a percentage of 400 = $\frac{209}{400}$ × 100 = 52.25%.

   N.B. if x is bigger than y you'll get a percentage that's bigger than 100.

3) Finding the $\underline{\text{percentage change}}$ is a bit trickier
   — you need to use this $\underline{\text{formula}}$:
   You end up with a $\underline{\text{percentage}}$ rather than
   an amount — e.g. a percentage $\underline{\text{increase}}$/$\underline{\text{profit}}$/$\underline{\text{error}}$ or a percentage $\underline{\text{decrease}}$/$\underline{\text{loss}}$/$\underline{\text{discount}}$.

$$\text{PERCENTAGE 'CHANGE'} = \frac{\text{'CHANGE'}}{\text{ORIGINAL}} \times 100$$

EXAMPLE: A trader buys 6 watches at £25 each. He scratches one of them, so he sells that one for £11. He sells the other five for £38 each. Find his profit as a percentage.

1) Here the 'change' is $\underline{\text{profit}}$, so the formula looks like this: percentage profit = $\frac{\text{profit}}{\text{original}}$ × 100

2) Work out the $\underline{\text{actual}}$ profit
   (amount made − amount spent):
   profit = (38 × 5) + 11 − (6 × 25)
   = £51

3) Calculate the $\underline{\text{percentage}}$ profit:
   percentage profit = $\frac{51}{6 \times 25}$ × 100 = 34%

Find a Decimal to Represent the Percentage Change

To find the $\underline{\text{new amount}}$ after a $\underline{\text{percentage increase}}$ or $\underline{\text{decrease}}$, you first need to find the $\underline{\text{multiplier}}$
— the decimal that represents the $\underline{\text{percentage change}}$.

E.g. 5% increase is 1.05 (= 1 + 0.05)
   26% decrease is 0.74 (= 1 − 0.26)

A % increase has a multiplier greater than 1, a % decrease has a multiplier less than 1.

Then you just $\underline{\text{multiply}}$ the $\underline{\text{original value}}$ by the $\underline{\text{multiplier}}$ and voilà — you have the answer.

EXAMPLE: A toaster is £38 excluding VAT. VAT is paid at 20%. What is the price of the toaster including VAT?

1) Find the $\underline{\text{multiplier}}$:   20% increase = 1 + 0.2 = 1.2

2) $\underline{\text{Multiply}}$ the $\underline{\text{original value}}$
   by the multiplier: 38 × 1.2 = £45.60

If you prefer, you can work out the **percentage**, then **add** or **subtract** it from the **original value**:
20% of £38 = 0.2 × 38 = £7.60
£38 + £7.60 = £45.60

EXAMPLE: A new school opened with 400 pupils. The number of pupils decreased by 5% by the end of the first year. By the end of the second year, the number of pupils had decreased by a further 10%. How many pupils were left in the school by the end of the second year?

1) After the $\underline{\text{first year}}$ there were: 400 × 0.95 = 380 pupils

2) After the $\underline{\text{second year}}$ there were 380 × 0.9 = 342 pupils

The multiplier is 1 − 0.05 = 0.95

The multiplier is 1 − 0.1 = 0.9 — and you have to use the amount you've just calculated as the new original value.

Make sure you're 100% confident with percentages...

Finding the multiplier is going to come in very handy on the next page, but first, try this question:

Q1   A house is put up for sale at £160 000. After 3 months, the price is decreased by 2.5%. After
   3 more months, it is decreased by a further 2%. What is the price after 6 months?   [3 marks]

Compound Growth and Decay

In <u>compound growth</u> or <u>decay</u>, an amount changes by a certain percentage at <u>regular intervals</u> (e.g. months, years, etc.). Each change is a percentage of the <u>new amount</u>, rather than the <u>original amount</u>.

Learn the Formula for Compound Growth/Decay

This topic is simple if you <u>LEARN THIS FORMULA</u>. If you don't, it's pretty well impossible:

Amount after n days/hours/years

$$N = N_0 \times (\text{multiplier})^n$$

Number of days/hours/years

Initial amount

Percentage change multiplier
E.g.   5% increase is 1.05 (= 1 + 0.05)
        26% decrease is 0.74 (= 1 − 0.26)

3 Examples to show you how EASY it is:

<u>Appreciation</u> questions are about things which <u>increase in value</u> over time (e.g. houses).
With <u>compound interest</u> questions, the amount in the account will <u>increase</u>, as interest is paid each year.
The amount of interest <u>increases</u> each year, as it's the <u>same percentage</u> of a <u>larger original value</u>.

EXAMPLE: Daniel invests £1000 in a savings account which pays 8% compound interest per annum. How much will there be after 6 years?

> 'Per annum' just means 'each year'.

Use the <u>formula</u>:   Amount = 1000 × (1.08)⁶ = £1586.87 (to the nearest penny)
initial amount ⟋   8% increase ⟍ 6 years

Amount $= 1000 \times (1.08)^6 = £1586.87$ (to the nearest penny)

<u>Depreciation</u> questions are about things which <u>decrease in value</u> over time (e.g. cars).

EXAMPLE: Susan has just bought a car for £6500.

a) If the car's value depreciates by 9% each year, how much will the car be worth in 3 years' time?
Use the <u>formula</u>:   Value $= 6500 \times (0.91)^3 = £4898.21$ (to the nearest penny)

b) How many complete years will it be before the car is worth less than £3000?

Use the <u>formula</u> again but this time you don't know <u>n</u>.

$$\text{Value} = 6500 \times (0.91)^n$$

Use <u>trial and error</u> to find how many years it will be before the value drops below £3000.

If $n = 8$, $6500 \times (0.91)^8 = 3056.6414....$
$n = 9$, $6500 \times (0.91)^9 = 2781.5437...$
It will be 9 years before the car is worth less than £3000.

The compound growth and decay formula can be used for other contexts, e.g. <u>population</u> and <u>disease</u>.

EXAMPLE: The number of bacteria in a sample increases at a rate of 30% each day. In the original sample, there were 1500 bacteria. How many bacteria will there be after 7 days?

Put the numbers you know into the <u>formula</u>:   Bacteria $= 1500 \times (1.3)^7$
$= 9412.277...$

<u>Round</u> the answer to the nearest whole number.   So there will be 9412 bacteria after 7 days.

I thought you'd appreciate all the work I've put into this page...

This page is all about the formula really, so make sure you learn it... learn it real good. Oh, and try this:

Q1   Alasdair's monthly rent is £600. His landlord is going to increase the monthly rent by 3.5% each year for the next 4 years. How much will Alasdair's monthly rent be in the 4th year?   [3 marks]

Reverse Percentages

One final page on percentages — and this time you get to do things in reverse (oooo...).

Reverse Percentages *Find the Original Value*

In a reverse percentage question, you're given the amount after a percentage increase or decrease, and asked to find the original amount. All you have to do is follow this simple method:

> 1) Write the amount in the question as a **percentage of the original value.**
> 2) **Divide** to find **1%** of the original value.
> 3) **Multiply by 100** to give the original value (= 100%).

EXAMPLE: A house increases in value by 10.5% to £132 600. Find what it was worth before the rise.

Note: The new, not the original value is given.

1) An increase of 10.5% means £132 600 represents 110.5% of the original value.

2) Divide by 110.5 to find 1% of the original value.

3) Then multiply by 100.

$÷110.5$ { £132 600 = 110.5%
£1200 = 1%
$×100$ { £120 000 = 100%

So the original value was £120 000

If it was a decrease of 10.5%, then you'd put '£132 600 = 89.5%' and divide by 89.5 instead of 110.5.

Always set them out exactly like this example. The trickiest bit is deciding the top % figure on the right-hand side — the 2nd and 3rd rows are always 1% and 100%. Here are two more examples:

EXAMPLE: A TV costs £450, including VAT. The rate of VAT is 20%. Find the price of the TV before VAT was added.

1) The price includes VAT, so it represents 100% + 20% = 120% of the price before VAT.

2) Divide by 120 to find 1% of the price before VAT.

3) Then multiply by 100.

$÷120$ { £450 = 120%
£3.75 = 1%
$×100$ { £375 = 100%

So the price before VAT was £375

EXAMPLE: A coat has been reduced by 12% in a sale. Its sale price is £74.80. Calculate the original price of the coat.

1) The sale price represents 100% − 12% = 88% of the original price.

2) Divide by 88 to find 1% of the original price.

3) Then multiply by 100.

This is a percentage decrease, so the sale value represents less than 100% of the original value.

$÷88$ { £74.80 = 88%
£0.85 = 1%
$×100$ { £85 = 100%

So the original price was £85

Caution — percentages reversing...

The method above is easy to follow — try it out for yourself on these Practice Questions:

Q1 A soft drinks company has decreased the amount of cordial in a bottle by 25%. There is now 900 ml of cordial in a bottle. Calculate the original amount of cordial in a bottle. [3 marks]

Q2 Lucy's kitten has a mass of 1500 g. Its mass has increased by 42% over the last month. What was its mass one month ago? Give your answer to the nearest gram. [3 marks]

The Laws of Indices

'Index' (plural: indices) is just another word for 'power'. Indices are a very useful shorthand:

$$2\times2\times2\times2\times2\times2\times2 = 2^7 \text{ ('two to the power 7' or '2 with index 7')}$$

That bit is easy to remember. Unfortunately, there are also ten special rules for indices that you need to learn.

The Seven Easy Rules:

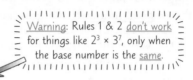

Warning: Rules 1 & 2 don't work for things like $2^3 \times 3^7$, only when the base number is the same.

1) When MULTIPLYING, you ADD THE INDICES.
e.g. $3^6 \times 3^4 = 3^{6+4} = 3^{10}$, $a^2 \times a^7 = a^{2+7} = a^9$

2) When DIVIDING, you SUBTRACT THE INDICES.
e.g. $5^4 \div 5^2 = 5^{4-2} = 5^2$, $b^8 \div b^5 = b^{8-5} = b^3$

3) When RAISING one index to another, you MULTIPLY THEM.
e.g. $(3^2)^4 = 3^{2\times4} = 3^8$, $(c^3)^6 = c^{3\times6} = c^{18}$

4) $x^1 = x$, ANYTHING with INDEX 1 is just ITSELF.
e.g. $3^1 = 3$, $d \times d^3 = d^1 \times d^3 = d^{1+3} = d^4$

5) $x^0 = 1$, ANYTHING with INDEX 0 is just 1.
e.g. $5^0 = 1$, $67^0 = 1$, $p^0 = 1$

6) $1^x = 1$, 1 WITH ANY INDEX is STILL JUST 1.
e.g. $1^{23} = 1$, $1^{89} = 1$, $1^2 = 1$

7) FRACTIONS — Apply the index to both TOP and BOTTOM.
e.g. $\left(1\frac{3}{5}\right)^3 = \left(\frac{8}{5}\right)^3 = \frac{8^3}{5^3} = \frac{512}{125}$, $\left(\frac{u}{v}\right)^5 = \frac{u^5}{v^5}$

EXAMPLE: Simplify $(3a^2b^4c)^3$

Just deal with each bit separately:
$$= (3)^3 \times (a^2)^3 \times (b^4)^3 \times (c)^3$$
$$= 27 \times a^{2\times3} \times b^{4\times3} \times c^3$$
$$= 27a^6b^{12}c^3$$

EXAMPLE: Simplify $\frac{a^8 \times 6a^4}{3a^5}$

Simplify the top of the fraction first, then divide:
$$= \frac{6a^{8+4}}{3a^5} = \frac{6a^{12}}{3a^5} = \frac{6}{3}a^{12-5} = 2a^7$$

The Three Tricky Rules:

8) NEGATIVE INDICES — Turn it Upside-Down

People have real difficulty remembering this — whenever you see a negative index you need to immediately think: "Aha, that means turn it the other way up and make the index positive".

e.g. $7^{-2} = \frac{1}{7^2} = \frac{1}{49}$, $a^{-4} = \frac{1}{a^4}$, $\left(\frac{3}{5}\right)^{-2} = \left(\frac{5}{3}\right)^{+2} = \frac{5^2}{3^2} = \frac{25}{9}$

9) FRACTIONAL INDICES

| The index $\frac{1}{2}$ means Square Root, |
| The index $\frac{1}{3}$ means Cube Root, |
| The index $\frac{1}{4}$ means Fourth Root etc. |

e.g. $25^{\frac{1}{2}} = \sqrt{25} = 5$
$64^{\frac{1}{3}} = \sqrt[3]{64} = 4$
$81^{\frac{1}{4}} = \sqrt[4]{81} = 3$
$z^{\frac{1}{5}} = \sqrt[5]{z}$

The one to really watch is when you get a negative fraction like $49^{-\frac{1}{2}}$ — people get mixed up and think that the minus is the square root, and forget to turn it upside down as well.

10) TWO-STAGE FRACTIONAL INDICES

With fractional indices like $64^{\frac{5}{6}}$ always split the fraction into a root and a power, and do them in that order: root first, then power: $(64)^{\frac{1}{6}\times5} = (64^{\frac{1}{6}})^5 = (2)^5 = 32$.

Don't let the power go to your head...

Learn all ten exciting rules on this page, then have a go at these Exam Practice Questions.

Q1 Simplify: a) $(g^6)^{\frac{1}{2}} \times g^2$ [1 mark] b) $2h^5j^{-2} \times 3h^2j^4$ [2 marks]

Q2 Evaluate without a calculator:

a) $625^{\frac{3}{4}}$ [2 marks] b) $25^{-\frac{1}{2}}$ [2 marks] c) $\left(\frac{27}{64}\right)^{-\frac{1}{3}}$ [2 marks]

Scientific Notation

Scientific notation (also called standard form) is useful for writing VERY BIG or VERY SMALL numbers in a more convenient way, e.g.

$56\,000\,000\,000$ would be 5.6×10^{10} in scientific notation.

$0.000\,000\,003\,45$ would be 3.45×10^{-9} in scientific notation.

But ANY NUMBER can be written in scientific notation and you need to know how to do it:

What it *Actually* is:

A number written in scientific notation must always be in exactly this form:

This number must always be between 1 and 10.

(The fancy way of saying this is $1 \le A < 10$)

$$A \times 10^n$$

This number is just the number of places the decimal point moves.

The decimal point doesn't actually move — the digits move around it. But thinking of it this way can be easier to get your head around.

Learn the Three Rules:

1) The front number must always be between 1 and 10.
2) The power of 10, n, is how far the decimal point moves.
3) n is positive for BIG numbers, n is negative for SMALL numbers.

(This is much better than rules based on which way the decimal point moves.)

Four Important Examples:

1 The population of a town is 35 600. Express this number in scientific notation.

1) Move the decimal point until 35 600 becomes 3.56 ($1 \le A < 10$)
2) The decimal point has moved 4 places so n = 4, giving: 10^4
3) 35 600 is a big number so n is +4, not −4

$3\,5\,6\,0\,0.0$

$= 3.56 \times 10^4$

2 Express 0.0000623 in scientific notation.

1) The decimal point must move 5 places to give 6.23 ($1 \le A < 10$). So the power of 10 is 5.
2) Since 0.0000623 is a small number it must be 10^{-5} not 10^{+5}

$0.0\,0\,0\,0\,6\,2\,3$

$= 6.23 \times 10^{-5}$

3 The mass of a grain of salt is 4.95×10^{-3} g. Give the mass as an ordinary number.

1) The power of 10 is negative, so it's a small number — the answer will be less than 1.
2) The power is −3, so the decimal point moves 3 places.

$0\,0\,0\,4.9\,5 \times 10^{-3}$

$= 0.00495$ g

4 What is 146.3 million in scientific notation?

Too many people get this type of question wrong. Just take your time and do it in two stages:

146.3 million $= 146.3 \times 1\,000\,000$

$= 146\,300\,000$ —— 1) Write the number out in full.

$= 1.463 \times 10^8$ —— 2) Convert to scientific notation.

The two favourite wrong answers for this are:

146.3×10^6 — which is kind of right but it's not in scientific notation because 146.3 is not between 1 and 10

1.463×10^6 — this one is in scientific notation but it's not big enough

Scientific Notation

Calculations with Scientific Notation

Multiplying and Dividing — not too bad

1) Rearrange to put the <u>front numbers</u> and the <u>powers of 10 together</u>.
2) Multiply or divide the front numbers, and use the <u>laws of indices</u> (see p.8) to multiply or divide the powers of 10.
3) Make sure your answer is still in <u>scientific notation</u>.

These questions could come up on the non-calculator paper, so make sure you know how to do them without using a calculator.

EXAMPLES:

1. Find $(2 \times 10^3) \times (6.75 \times 10^5)$ without using a calculator.
Give your answer in scientific notation.

Multiply front numbers and powers separately

$$(2 \times 10^3) \times (6.75 \times 10^5)$$
$$= (2 \times 6.75) \times (10^3 \times 10^5)$$
$$= 13.5 \times 10^{3+5} \quad \text{—— Add the indices (see p.8)}$$
$$= 13.5 \times 10^8$$

Not in scientific notation — convert it
$$= 1.35 \times 10 \times 10^8$$
$$= 1.35 \times 10^9$$

2. A province of a mountainous country has a population of 240 000 and an area of (4.8×10^{10}) m². Find the number of people per square metre, giving your answer in scientific notation.

The calculation you need to do is:

$$240\ 000 \div (4.8 \times 10^{10})$$

Convert 240 000 to scientific notation
$$= \frac{2.4 \times 10^5}{4.8 \times 10^{10}} = \frac{2.4}{4.8} \times \frac{10^5}{10^{10}}$$

Divide front numbers and powers separately
$$= 0.5 \times 10^{5-10} \quad \text{—— Subtract the indices}$$
$$= 0.5 \times 10^{-5} \quad \text{(see p.8)}$$

Not in scientific notation — convert it
$$= 5 \times 10^{-1} \times 10^{-5}$$
$$= 5 \times 10^{-6} \text{ people per m}^2$$

Adding and Subtracting — a bit trickier

1) Make sure the <u>powers of 10</u> are <u>the same</u> — you'll probably need to rewrite one of them.
2) Add or subtract the <u>front numbers</u>.
3) Convert the answer to <u>scientific notation</u> if necessary.

EXAMPLE:

Calculate $(9.8 \times 10^4) + (6.6 \times 10^3)$ without using a calculator.
Give your answer in scientific notation.

$$(9.8 \times 10^4) + (6.6 \times 10^3)$$

1) <u>Rewrite one number</u> so both powers of 10 are equal: $\quad = (9.8 \times 10^4) + (0.66 \times 10^4)$
2) Now add the <u>front numbers</u>: $\quad = (9.8 + 0.66) \times 10^4$
3) 10.46×10^4 isn't in scientific notation, so <u>convert it</u>: $\quad = 10.46 \times 10^4 = 1.046 \times 10^5$

To put numbers in scientific notation into your <u>calculator</u>, use the `EXP` or the `×10ˣ` button.
E.g. enter 2.67×10^{15} by pressing `2.67` `EXP` `15` `=` or `2.67` `×10ˣ` `15` `=` .

My work rate is 5×10^{-2} pages per hour...

Make sure you understand all the examples on these two pages. Then try this Exam Practice Question:

Q1 40 grains of rice weigh 1 g. A catering company uses 60 kg of rice at a food festival.
Without using a calculator, work out how many grains of rice they use.
Give your answer in scientific notation.

[2 marks]

Manipulating Surds

Surds are expressions with irrational square roots in them (irrational numbers are ones which can't be written as fractions, such as most square roots, cube roots and π). So $\sqrt{2}$ is irrational, but $\sqrt{4} = 2$ is not.

Manipulating Surds — 6 Rules to Learn

There are 6 rules you need to learn for dealing with surds...

1 $\sqrt{a} \times \sqrt{b} = \sqrt{a \times b}$ e.g. $\sqrt{2} \times \sqrt{3} = \sqrt{2 \times 3} = \sqrt{6}$ — also $(\sqrt{b})^2 = \sqrt{b} \times \sqrt{b} = \sqrt{b \times b} = b$

2 $\dfrac{\sqrt{a}}{\sqrt{b}} = \sqrt{\dfrac{a}{b}}$ e.g. $\dfrac{\sqrt{8}}{\sqrt{2}} = \sqrt{\dfrac{8}{2}} = \sqrt{4} = 2$

3 $\sqrt{a} + \sqrt{b}$ — __DO NOTHING__ — in other words it is definitely $\underline{NOT}$ $\sqrt{a+b}$

4 $(a + \sqrt{b})^2 = (a + \sqrt{b})(a + \sqrt{b}) = a^2 + 2a\sqrt{b} + b$ — $\underline{NOT}$ just $a^2 + (\sqrt{b})^2$ (see p.13)

5 $(a + \sqrt{b})(a - \sqrt{b}) = a^2 + a\sqrt{b} - a\sqrt{b} - (\sqrt{b})^2 = a^2 - b$ (see p.13).

6 $\dfrac{a}{\sqrt{b}} = \dfrac{a}{\sqrt{b}} \times \dfrac{\sqrt{b}}{\sqrt{b}} = \dfrac{a\sqrt{b}}{b}$ This is known as 'RATIONALISING the denominator' — it's where you get rid of the $\sqrt{}$ on the bottom of the fraction (see example 3 below).

Use the Rules to Simplify Expressions

EXAMPLES: **1.** Write $\sqrt{300} + \sqrt{48} - 2\sqrt{75}$ in the form $a\sqrt{3}$, where a is an integer.

Write each surd in terms of $\sqrt{3}$: $\sqrt{300} = \sqrt{100 \times 3} = \sqrt{100} \times \sqrt{3} = 10\sqrt{3}$

$\sqrt{48} = \sqrt{16 \times 3} = \sqrt{16} \times \sqrt{3} = 4\sqrt{3}$

$2\sqrt{75} = 2\sqrt{25 \times 3} = 2 \times \sqrt{25} \times \sqrt{3} = 10\sqrt{3}$

Then do the sum (leaving your answer in terms of $\sqrt{3}$):

$$\sqrt{300} + \sqrt{48} - 2\sqrt{75} = 10\sqrt{3} + 4\sqrt{3} - 10\sqrt{3} = 4\sqrt{3}$$

2. A rectangle with length $4x$ cm and width x cm has an area of 32 cm². Find the exact value of x, giving your answer in its simplest form.

Area of rectangle = length × width = $4x \times x = 4x^2$

So $4x^2 = 32$
$x^2 = 8$ You can ignore the negative square root as length must be positive.
$x = \pm\sqrt{8}$

'Exact value' means you have to leave your answer in surd form, so get $\sqrt{8}$ into its simplest form:
$\sqrt{8} = \sqrt{4 \times 2} = \sqrt{4}\sqrt{2}$
$= 2\sqrt{2}$ So $x = 2\sqrt{2}$

3. Write $\dfrac{18}{\sqrt{12}}$ in the form $a\sqrt{b}$, where a and b are integers. Give your answer in its simplest form.

To rationalise the denominator, multiply top and bottom by $\sqrt{12}$:

$$\dfrac{18}{\sqrt{12}} = \dfrac{18\sqrt{12}}{12} = \dfrac{3\sqrt{4 \times 3}}{2}$$

$$= \dfrac{3 \times 2 \times \sqrt{3}}{2} = \dfrac{6\sqrt{3}}{2}$$

$$= 3\sqrt{3} \text{ (so } a = 3 \text{ and } b = 3)$$

Rationalise the denominator? How absurd...

Learn the 6 rules for manipulating surds, then give these Exam Practice Questions a go...

Q1   Write $\sqrt{162} - \sqrt{72}$ in the form $a\sqrt{b}$, where a and b are integers to be found.   [3 marks]

Q2   Write $\dfrac{9}{\sqrt{18}}$ as a fraction with a rational denominator in its simplest form.   [3 marks]

Revision Questions for Section One

Well, that wraps up <u>Section One</u> — time to put yourself to the test and find out <u>how much you really know</u>.
- Try these questions and <u>tick off each one</u> when you <u>get it right</u>.
- When you've done <u>all the questions</u> for a topic and are <u>completely happy</u> with it, tick off the topic.

Fractions and Rounding (p2-4) ☑

You're <u>not allowed</u> to use a <u>calculator</u> for q1-6, 16, 18 and 21-27. Sorry.

1) How do you simplify a fraction?
2) a) Write $\frac{74}{9}$ as a mixed number   b) Write $4\frac{5}{7}$ as an improper fraction
3) a) Find $\frac{7}{9}$ of 270 kg.   b) Write 88 as a fraction of 56.
4) What are the rules for multiplying, dividing and adding/subtracting fractions?
5) Calculate: a) $\frac{2}{11} \times \frac{7}{9}$ b) $5\frac{1}{2} \div 1\frac{3}{4}$ c) $\frac{5}{8} - \frac{1}{6}$ d) $3\frac{3}{10} + 4\frac{1}{4}$
6) Calculate $\frac{6}{5}\left(\frac{2}{3} - \frac{1}{8}\right)$.
7) Round 427.963 to: a) 2 d.p.   b) 1 d.p.   c) 2 s.f.   d) 4 s.f.
8) Round 0.00178423 to 3 significant figures.

Percentages (p5-7) ☑

9) If $x = 20$ and $y = 95$:   a) Find x% of y.   b) Express y as a percentage of x.
10) What's the formula for finding a change in value as a percentage?
11) An antique wardrobe decreased in value from £800 to £520. What was the percentage decrease?
12) Mila bought a statue for £2520. It has increased in value by 18%. What is it worth now?
13) What's the formula for compound growth and decay?
14) Collectable baseball cards increase in value by 7% each year. A particular card is worth £80.
    a) How much will it be worth in 10 years?   b) In how many years will it be worth over £200?
15) A tree's height has increased by 15% in the last year to 20.24 m. What was its height a year ago?
16) Toby has sold 260 football stickers, which is 65% of the football stickers that were in his collection. How many football stickers were in his collection?

Laws of Indices and Scientific Notation (p8-10) ☑

17) Simplify the following: a) $x^3 \times x^6$ b) $y^7 \div y^5$ c) $(z^3)^4$
18) Work out the value of: a) $225^{\frac{1}{2}}$ b) $36^{-\frac{1}{2}}$ c) $8^{\frac{4}{3}}$
19) Write $\frac{1}{\sqrt[4]{a}}$ in the form a^b.
20) What are the three rules for writing numbers in scientific notation?
21) Write these numbers in scientific notation:
    a) 970 000   b) 3 560 000 000   c) 0.00000275
22) Express 4.56×10^{-3} and 2.7×10^5 as ordinary numbers.
23) Calculate: a) $(3.2 \times 10^6) \div (1.6 \times 10^3)$ b) $(1.75 \times 10^{12}) + (9.89 \times 10^{11})$
    Give your answers in scientific notation.
24) At the start of an experiment, there are 3.1×10^8 bacteria on a petri dish. The number of bacteria doubles every 10 minutes. How many bacteria will there be after 30 minutes?

Manipulating Surds (p11) ☑

25) Simplify the following: a) $\sqrt{27}$ b) $\sqrt{125} \div \sqrt{5}$
26) Write $\sqrt{98} + 3\sqrt{8} - \sqrt{200}$ in the form $a\sqrt{2}$, where a is an integer.
27) Rationalise the denominators of: a) $\frac{2}{\sqrt{7}}$ b) $\frac{4}{\sqrt{12}}$

Expanding Brackets

I usually use brackets to make witty comments (I'm very witty), but in algebra they're useful for simplifying things. First of all, you need to know how to expand brackets (multiply them out).

Single *Brackets*

The main thing to remember when multiplying out brackets is that the thing **outside** the bracket multiplies **each separate term** inside the bracket.

EXAMPLE: Expand the following:

a) $4a(3a - 2b)$

$= (4a \times 3a) + (4a \times -2b)$
$= 12a^2 - 8ab$

b) $-p(6 - 7p)$

$= (-p \times 6) + (-p \times -7p)$
$= -6p + 7p^2$

Note: both signs have been reversed.

Double *Brackets*

Double brackets are trickier than single brackets — this time, you have to multiply **everything** in the **first bracket** by **everything** in the **second bracket**. You'll get **4 terms**, and usually 2 of them will combine to leave **3 terms**. There's a handy way to multiply out double brackets — it's called the **FOIL method**:

First — multiply the first term in each bracket together
Outside — multiply the outside terms (i.e. the first term in the first bracket by the second term in the second bracket)
Inside — multiply the inside terms (i.e. the second term in the first bracket by the first term in the second bracket)
Last — multiply the second term in each bracket together

EXAMPLE: Expand and simplify $(2p - 4)(3p + 1)$

$(2p - 4)(3p + 1) = (2p \times 3p) + (2p \times 1) + (-4 \times 3p) + (-4 \times 1)$
$\qquad\qquad\qquad = \quad 6p^2 \quad + \quad 2p \quad - 12p \quad - 4$
$\qquad\qquad\qquad = \quad 6p^2 - 10p - 4$

The two p terms combine together.

Always write out **SQUARED BRACKETS** as **TWO BRACKETS** (to avoid mistakes), then multiply out as above.
So $(3x + 5)^2 = (3x + 5)(3x + 5) = 9x^2 + 15x + 15x + 25 = 9x^2 + 30x + 25$.
(DON'T make the mistake of thinking that $(3x + 5)^2 = 9x^2 + 25$ — this is **wrong wrong wrong**.)

Sometimes there'll be **more than two** terms in a bracket — just make sure you multiply **every term** in one bracket by **every term** in the other bracket.

EXAMPLE: Expand and simplify $(2x + 3)(-2x^2 - 9x + 10)$

Be extra careful with the negative terms.

$(2x + 3)(-2x^2 - 9x + 10) = 2x(-2x^2 - 9x + 10) + 3(-2x^2 - 9x + 10)$
$\qquad\qquad\qquad\qquad = (2x \times -2x^2) + (2x \times -9x) + (2x \times 10)$
$\qquad\qquad\qquad\qquad\qquad\qquad + (3 \times -2x^2) + (3 \times -9x) + (3 \times 10)$
$\qquad\qquad\qquad\qquad = -4x^3 + -18x^2 + 20x + -6x^2 + -27x + 30$
$\qquad\qquad\qquad\qquad = -4x^3 - 24x^2 - 7x + 30$

Go forth and multiply out brackets...

After you've multiplied out the brackets, don't forget to tidy everything up and collect terms that have the same power of x — you're likely to lose a mark in the exam if you don't.

Q1   Expand and simplify: a) $(y + 4)(y - 5)$ [2 marks]   b) $(2p - 3)^2$ [2 marks]

Q2   Expand and simplify: a) $(x - 2)(4x^2 - x + 2)$ [3 marks]   b) $(x^2 - x + 9)(x + 1)$ [3 marks]

Expanding Brackets

One more page on expanding brackets — now it's time for sums of brackets and writing your own expressions.

Sums of Brackets

If you've <u>mastered</u> all the other stuff, then this will be a <u>breeze</u>. If you have a <u>sum</u> of sets of brackets (e.g. $4(x + 2) + 3(x - 1)$ or $(x + 2)^2 + (x - 1)(x + 3)$), always <u>multiply out</u> each set of brackets <u>first</u>. Then you can <u>add</u> them all together and <u>collect like terms</u> to tidy up.

EXAMPLE: Expand and simplify $2x(8 - 3x) + (4x - 1)(2x - 3)$.

Use FOIL on the second bracket.

$2x(8 - 3x) + (4x - 1)(2x - 3) = 16x - 6x^2 + (8x^2 - 12x - 2x + 3)$

Expand the first bracket.

$= 16x - 6x^2 + 8x^2 - 14x + 3$
$= 2x^2 + 2x + 3$

You Might Have to Find Your Own Expressions

In an exam question, you might be given some <u>information</u> which you have to use to <u>set up</u> an expression involving <u>brackets</u>. You'll then have to <u>expand</u> the brackets and <u>collect like terms</u> to simplify it. This type of thing can come up in <u>shape</u> questions, so make sure you're happy with <u>perimeter</u> and <u>area</u>.

EXAMPLE: Lucy has sketched the front of her house. The sketch is made up of a rectangle and a trapezium, as shown in the diagram.

All measurements are in centimetres.

Find an expression for the total area of the sketch.

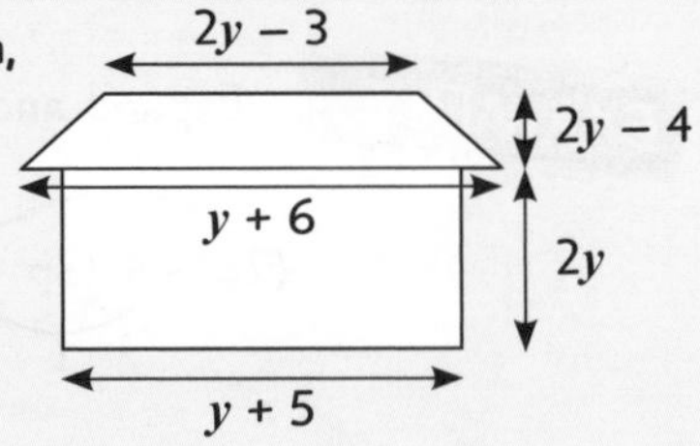

$2y - 3$, $2y - 4$, $y + 6$, $2y$, $y + 5$

The <u>total area</u> of the sketch is:

Area of Rectangle + Area of Trapezium = $2y(y + 5) + \frac{1}{2}[(y + 6) + (2y - 3)](2y - 4)$

Multiply out each set of brackets first and then tidy up.

The area of a trapezium is $\frac{1}{2}(a + b) \times h$, where h is the height and a and b are its parallel sides.

The area of the <u>rectangle</u> is:

$2y(y + 5) = 2y^2 + 10y$

The area of the <u>trapezium</u> is:

$\frac{1}{2}[(y + 6) + (2y - 3)](2y - 4)$
$= \frac{1}{2}(3y + 3)(2y - 4)$
$= \frac{1}{2}(6y^2 - 12y + 6y - 12)$
$= \frac{1}{2}(6y^2 - 6y - 12)$
$= 3y^2 - 3y - 6$

So the <u>total area</u> is: $2y^2 + 10y + 3y^2 - 3y - 6 = 5y^2 + 7y - 6$ cm²

Don't brack it — you've got this...

Don't forget to tidy up your final answer by collecting like terms — otherwise you might lose a mark.

Q1 Expand and simplify: a) $2(x - 1) + 9(3x + 2)$ [2 marks] b) $2(p + q) - 3(p - 1)^2$ [3 marks]

Q2 A triangle has a base of $(2x + 4)$ cm and a vertical height of $(x^2 + 3x + 4)$ cm. Find an expression for the area of the triangle, giving your answer in its simplest form. [3 marks]

Section Two — Algebraic Skills

Factorising

Right, now you know how to expand brackets, it's time to put them back in. This is known as <u>factorising</u>.

Factorising — Putting Brackets In

This is the <u>exact reverse</u> of multiplying out brackets. Here's the method to follow:

1) Take out the <u>biggest number</u> that goes into all the terms.
2) <u>For each letter in turn</u>, take out the <u>highest power</u> (e.g. x, x^2 etc.) that will go into **EVERY** term.
3) Open the bracket and fill in all the bits needed to <u>reproduce each term</u>.
4) <u>Check</u> your answer by <u>multiplying out</u> the bracket and making sure it matches the original expression.

EXAMPLES:

1. Factorise $3x^2 + 6x$

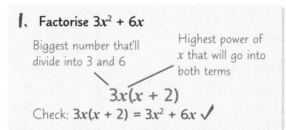

Biggest number that'll divide into 3 and 6

Highest power of x that will go into both terms

$3x(x + 2)$

Check: $3x(x + 2) = 3x^2 + 6x$ ✓

2. Factorise $8x^2y + 2xy^2$

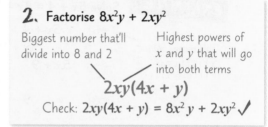

Biggest number that'll divide into 8 and 2

Highest powers of x and y that will go into both terms

$2xy(4x + y)$

Check: $2xy(4x + y) = 8x^2y + 2xy^2$ ✓

<u>REMEMBER</u>: The bits <u>taken out</u> and put at the front are the <u>common factors</u>. The bits <u>inside the bracket</u> are what's needed to get back to the <u>original terms</u> if you multiply the bracket out again.

D.O.T.S. — The Difference Of Two Squares

The 'difference of two squares' (D.O.T.S. for short) is where you have 'one thing squared' <u>take away</u> 'another thing squared'. There's a quick and easy way to factorise it — just use the rule below:

$$a^2 - b^2 = (a + b)(a - b)$$

EXAMPLE:

Factorise:

a) $x^2 - 49$

Answer: $x^2 - 49 = (x + 7)(x - 7)$
$49 = 7^2$ so $+7$ and -7 go in the brackets

b) $9p^2 - 16q^2$

Answer: $9p^2 - 16q^2 = (3p + 4q)(3p - 4q)$
Here you had to spot that 9 and 16 are square numbers.

c) $3x^2 - 75y^2$

Answer: $3x^2 - 75y^2 = 3(x^2 - 25y^2) = 3(x + 5y)(x - 5y)$
This time, you had to take out a factor of 3 first.

Watch out — the difference of two squares can creep into other <u>algebra questions</u>. You might come across a difference of two squares on the top or bottom of a <u>fraction</u> and ask you to simplify it. There's more on algebraic fractions on p.31.

EXAMPLE:

Simplify $\dfrac{x^2 - 36}{5x + 30}$

The numerator is a difference of two squares.

$$\frac{x^2 - 36}{5x + 30} = \frac{(x + 6)(x - 6)}{5(x + 6)} = \frac{x - 6}{5}$$

Factorise the denominator.

Well, one's green and one's yellow...

As factorising is the reverse process of expanding brackets, you <u>must check</u> your answer by multiplying out the brackets. Make sure you can spot differences of two squares as well — they can be a bit sneaky.

Q1 Factorise $6xy + 15y^2$ [1 mark]

Q2 Factorise $x^2 - 16y^2$ [1 mark]

Q3 Factorise $20x^2 - 45y^2$ [2 marks]

Q4 Simplify $\dfrac{6x - 42}{x^2 - 49}$ [3 marks]

Solving Equations

The basic idea of <u>solving equations</u> is very simple — keep <u>rearranging</u> until you end up with x = number. The two most common methods for <u>rearranging</u> equations are: 1) '<u>same to both sides</u>' and 2) do the <u>opposite</u> when you cross the '='. We'll use the 'same to both sides' method on these pages.

Rearrange Until You Have x = Number

The easiest ones to solve are where you just have a <u>mixture</u> of x's and numbers.

1) First, <u>rearrange</u> the equation so that all the <u>x's</u> are on one side and the <u>numbers</u> are on the other. <u>Combine</u> terms where you can by <u>collecting like terms</u>.

2) Then <u>divide</u> both sides by the <u>number multiplying x</u> to find the value of x.

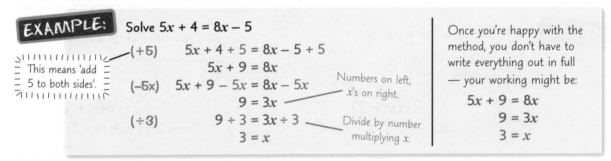

EXAMPLE: Solve $5x + 4 = 8x - 5$

This means 'add 5 to both sides'.

$(+5)$ $\quad 5x + 4 + 5 = 8x - 5 + 5$
$\quad\quad\quad\quad 5x + 9 = 8x$
$(-5x)$ $\quad 5x + 9 - 5x = 8x - 5x$ $\quad$ Numbers on left, x's on right.
$\quad\quad\quad\quad 9 = 3x$
$(\div 3)$ $\quad\quad 9 \div 3 = 3x \div 3$ $\quad$ Divide by number multiplying x.
$\quad\quad\quad\quad 3 = x$

Once you're happy with the method, you don't have to write everything out in full — your working might be:

$5x + 9 = 8x$
$9 = 3x$
$3 = x$

Multiply Out Brackets First

If your equation has <u>brackets</u> in it...

1) <u>Multiply</u> them out <u>before rearranging</u>.

2) <u>Solve it</u> in the same way as above.

EXAMPLE: Solve $3(3x - 2) = 5x + 10$

$\quad\quad\quad\quad 9x - 6 = 5x + 10$
$(-5x)$ $\quad 9x - 6 - 5x = 5x + 10 - 5x$
$\quad\quad\quad\quad 4x - 6 = 10$
$(+6)$ $\quad\quad 4x - 6 + 6 = 10 + 6$
$\quad\quad\quad\quad 4x = 16$
$(\div 4)$ $\quad\quad 4x \div 4 = 16 \div 4$
$\quad\quad\quad\quad x = 4$

Get Rid of Fractions (before they take over the world)

1) <u>Fractions</u> make everything more complicated — so you need to get rid of them <u>before doing anything else</u> (yep, even before multiplying out brackets).

2) To get rid of fractions, multiply <u>every term</u> of the equation by whatever's on the <u>bottom</u> of the fraction. If there are <u>two</u> fractions, you'll need to multiply by <u>both</u> denominators.

EXAMPLES:

1. Solve $\dfrac{x+2}{4} = 4x - 7$

$(\times 4)$ $\quad \dfrac{4(x+2)}{4} = 4(4x) - 4(7)$

Multiply <u>every term</u> by 4 to get rid of the fraction.

$\quad\quad x + 2 = 16x - 28$
$\quad\quad 30 = 15x$ —And solve.
$\quad\quad 2 = x$

2. Solve $\dfrac{3x+5}{2} = \dfrac{4x+10}{3}$

Multiply <u>everything</u> by 2 then by 3.

$(\times 2), (\times 3)$ $\quad \dfrac{2 \times 3 \times (3x+5)}{2} = \dfrac{2 \times 3 \times (4x+10)}{3}$

$\quad\quad 3(3x+5) = 2(4x+10)$

And solve.

$\quad\quad 9x + 15 = 8x + 20$
$\quad\quad x = 5$

Solving equations — more fun than greasing a seal...

Here's a handy final tip — you can always check your answer by sticking it in both sides of the original equation. They should both give the same number. Now practise what you've learned on these beauts:

Q1   Solve $2x + 5 = 17 - 4x$ [2 marks]

Q2   Solve $4(y + 3) = 3y + 16$ [2 marks]

Q3   Solve $\dfrac{3x+2}{5} = \dfrac{5x+6}{9}$ [3 marks]

Solving Equations

Now you know the basics of solving equations, it's time to put it together into a handy step-by-step method.

Solving Equations Using the 5-Step Method

Here's the method to follow (just ignore any steps that don't apply to your equation):

1) Get rid of any <u>fractions</u>.
2) <u>Multiply out</u> any brackets.
3) Collect all the <u>x-terms</u> on one side and all <u>number terms</u> on the other.
4) Reduce it to the form '<u>Ax = B</u>' (by <u>combining like terms</u>).
5) Finally <u>divide both sides by A</u> to give 'x =   ', and that's your answer.

EXAMPLE: Solve $\frac{3x+4}{5} + \frac{4x-1}{3} = 14$

Multiply everything by 5 then by 3.

1) **Get rid of any <u>fractions</u>.** (×5), (×3) $\frac{5\times3\times(3x+4)}{5} + \frac{5\times3\times(4x-1)}{3} = 5\times3\times14$

$$3(3x + 4) + 5(4x - 1) = 210$$

2) **<u>Multiply out</u> any brackets.** $9x + 12 + 20x - 5 = 210$

3) **Collect all the <u>x-terms</u> on one side and all <u>number terms</u> on the other.**

(−12), (+5) $9x + 20x = 210 - 12 + 5$

4) **Reduce it to the form '<u>Ax = B</u>' (by <u>combining like terms</u>).** $29x = 203$

5) **Finally <u>divide both sides by A</u> to give 'x =   ', and that's your answer.**

(÷29) $x = 7$

You might even have to <u>set up</u> your own equation from a <u>situation</u> given in <u>words</u>.

EXAMPLE: A baker makes jam tarts. In the kitchen, there are five full trays of tarts and 9 single tarts. In the shop, there are 3 full shelves of tarts. Each shelf contains 7 more tarts than a tray.
If the number of tarts in the kitchen is equal to the number of tarts in the shop, how many tarts fit on one tray?

First, <u>set up your equation</u> — you need to <u>find expressions</u> for the number of tarts in the kitchen and the number in the shop. Let x be the value <u>you're interested in</u> (the number of tarts on a tray).

1) In the <u>kitchen</u> there are $5x$ tarts, plus another 9 tarts: $(5x + 9)$
In the <u>shop</u>, one shelf holds 7 more tarts than a tray, so a shelf has $x + 7$ tarts on it. There are 3 of these: $3(x + 7)$

2) Now set your expressions <u>equal</u> to each other (as there are the same number of tarts in the kitchen and the shop) and <u>solve</u> to find x:

$(5x + 9) = 3(x + 7)$
$5x + 9 = 3x + 21$ —— Expand the brackets
$2x = 12$ —— Collect the x-terms
$x = 6$ —— Divide by 2   So 6 tarts fit on one tray.

You got all the questions right? That's a bit jammy...

If you have to set up your own equations, carefully go through and pick out all the relevant information. Write it all down and work out what equals what — then just apply the five step method to solve it.

Q1   Solve $\frac{2}{x} + 8 = \frac{82}{x}$ [3 marks]   Q2   Solve $\frac{3x-2}{2} - \frac{4x-5}{3} = 2$ [3 marks]

Inequalities

Inequalities aren't <u>half as difficult as they look</u>. Once you've learned the tricks involved, most of the algebra for them is <u>identical to ordinary equations</u> (have a look back at p.16-17 if you need a reminder).

The Inequality Symbols

> Inequalities are also known as <u>inequations</u>.

$>$ means '<u>Greater than</u>'	$\geq$ means '<u>Greater than or equal to</u>'
$<$ means '<u>Less than</u>'	$\leq$ means '<u>Less than or equal to</u>'

Algebra With Inequalities

The key thing about inequalities — solve them <u>just like regular equations</u> but <u>WITH ONE BIG EXCEPTION</u>:

Whenever you <u>MULTIPLY</u> OR <u>DIVIDE</u> by a <u>NEGATIVE NUMBER</u>, you must <u>FLIP THE INEQUALITY SIGN</u>.

EXAMPLES:

1. x is an integer such that $-4 < x \leq 3$.
Find all the possible values of x.

Work out what each bit of the inequality is telling you:

$-4 < x$ means 'x is greater than -4',
$x \leq 3$ means 'x is less than or equal to 3'.

Now just write down all the values that x can take.
(Remember, integers are just +ve or −ve whole numbers)

$$-3, -2, -1, 0, 1, 2, 3$$

2. Solve $6x + 7 > x + 22$.

Just solve it like an equation:

(-7) $6x + 7 - 7 > x + 22 - 7$
$6x > x + 15$

$(-x)$ $6x - x > x + 15 - x$
$5x > 15$

$(\div 5)$ $5x \div 5 > 15 \div 5$
$x > 3$

3. Solve $-2 \leq \dfrac{x}{4} + 3 \leq 5$.

Don't be put off because there are two inequality signs — just do the same thing to each bit of the inequality:

(-3) $-2 - 3 \leq \dfrac{x}{4} + 3 - 3 \leq 5 - 3$

$-5 \leq \dfrac{x}{4} \leq 2$

$(\times 4)$ $4 \times -5 \leq \dfrac{4 \times x}{4} \leq 4 \times 2$

$-20 \leq x \leq 8$

4. Solve $9 - 2x > 15$.

Again, solve it like an equation:

(-9) $9 - 2x - 9 > 15 - 9$
$-2x > 6$

$(\div -2)$ $-2x \div -2 < 6 \div -2$
$x < -3$

> The > has turned into a <, because we divided by a <u>negative number</u>.

5. Solve the inequation $5x + 3(x + 3) > 10x + 1$.

Expand any brackets first and then carry on as normal.

$5x + 3(x + 3) > 10x + 1$
$5x + 3x + 9 > 10x + 1$
$8x + 9 > 10x + 1$

$(-8x)$ $9 > 2x + 1$

(-1) $8 > 2x$

$(\div 2)$ $4 > x$

I > All of you.

I saw you flip the inequality sign — how rude...

To check you've got the inequality sign right, pop in a value for x and check the inequality's true.

Q1 Solve: a) $11x + 3 < 42 - 2x$ [2 marks]   b) $6 - 4x \geq 18$ [2 marks]

Q2 Solve, algebraically, the inequation $20 > 3x - 2(x + 2)$.   [3 marks]

Rearranging Formulas

Rearranging formulas means making one letter the subject, e.g. getting 'y = ' from '2x + z = 3(y + 2p)' — you have to get the subject on its own.

Rearrange Formulas *with the Solving Equations Method*

Rearranging formulas is remarkably similar to solving equations. The method below is identical to the method for solving equations, except that I've added a couple of extra steps.

1) Get rid of any square root signs by squaring both sides.
2) Get rid of any fractions.
3) Multiply out any brackets.
4) Collect all the subject terms on one side and all non-subject terms on the other.
5) Reduce it to the form '$Ax = B$' (by combining like terms). ← x is the subject term here. A and B could be numbers or letters (or a mix of both).
   You might have to do some factorising here too.
6) Divide both sides by A to give '$x = $ '.
7) If you're left with '$x^2 = $ ', square root both sides to get '$x = \pm$ ' (don't forget the ±).

What To Do If...

...the Subject Appears in a Fraction

You won't always need to use all 7 steps in the method above — just ignore the ones that don't apply.

EXAMPLE: Make b the subject of the formula $a = \dfrac{5b+3}{4}$.

There aren't any square roots, so ignore step 1.

2) Get rid of any fractions.	(by multiplying every term by 4, the denominator)	(×4) $4a = \dfrac{4(5b+3)}{4}$

$$4a = 5b + 3$$

There aren't any brackets so ignore step 3.

4) Collect all the subject terms on one side and all non-subject terms on the other.

(remember that you're trying to make b the subject)   (−3) $5b = 4a - 3$

5) It's now in the form $Ab = B$. (where A = 5 and B = 4a − 3)

6) Divide both sides by 5 to give '$b = $ '.   (÷5) $b = \dfrac{4a-3}{5}$

b isn't squared, so you don't need step 7.

If I could rearrange my subjects, I'd have maths all day...

Learn the 7 steps for rearranging formulas. Then get rearrangin' with these snazzy practice questions:

Q1 Make q the subject of the formula $p = \dfrac{q}{7} + 2r$. [2 marks]

Q2 The imperial formula for BMI, b, is $b = \dfrac{703w}{h^2}$, where w is weight in pounds and h is height in inches. Make w the subject. [2 marks]

Rearranging Formulas

Carrying straight on from the previous page, now it's time for what to do if...

...there's a *Square* or *Square Root Involved*

If the subject is a <u>square</u> or is in a <u>square root</u>, you have to use steps 1 and 7 (not necessarily both).

EXAMPLE: Make u the subject of the formula $v^2 = u^2 + 2as$.

There aren't any square roots, fractions or brackets so ignore steps 1-3 (this is pretty easy so far).

4) Collect all the <u>subject terms</u> on one side and all <u>non-subject terms</u> on the other.

$$(-2as) \quad u^2 = v^2 - 2as$$

> This is a real-life equation —
> v = final velocity, u = initial
> velocity, a = acceleration and
> s = displacement.

5) It's now in the form $\underline{Au^2 = B}$ (where $A = 1$ and $B = v^2 - 2as$)

$A = 1$, which means it's already in the form '$u^2 =$', so ignore step 6.

7) <u>Square root</u> both sides to get '$u = \pm$'. $(\sqrt{\ })$ $\quad u = \pm\sqrt{v^2 - 2as}$

EXAMPLE: Make n the subject of the formula $2(m + 3) = \sqrt{n + 5}$.

1) Get rid of any <u>square roots</u> by <u>squaring</u> both sides.
$$[2(m + 3)]^2 = (\sqrt{n + 5})^2$$
$$4(m^2 + 6m + 9) = n + 5$$

There aren't any fractions so ignore step 2.
$$4m^2 + 24m + 36 = n + 5$$

The brackets were removed when squaring so ignore step 3.

4) Collect all the <u>subject terms</u> on one side and all <u>non-subject terms</u> on the other.

$(-5) \quad n = 4m^2 + 24m + 31$ This is in the form '$n =$' so you don't need to do steps 5-7.

...the *Subject Appears Twice*

Go home and cry. No, not really — you'll just have to do some <u>factorising</u>, usually in step 5.

EXAMPLE: Make p the subject of the formula $q = \dfrac{p + 1}{p - 1}$.

There aren't any square roots so ignore step 1.

2) Get rid of any <u>fractions</u>. $q(p - 1) = p + 1$ | 3) <u>Multiply out</u> any brackets. $pq - q = p + 1$

4) Collect all the <u>subject terms</u> on one side and all <u>non-subject terms</u> on the other.

$$pq - p = q + 1$$

5) <u>Combine like terms</u> on each side of the equation. $p(q - 1) = q + 1$

> This is where you factorise —
> p was in both terms on the LHS
> so it comes out as a common factor.

6) <u>Divide both sides by $(q - 1)$</u> to give '$p =$'. $p = \dfrac{q + 1}{q - 1}$ (p isn't squared, so you don't need step 7.)

...there's a pirate invasion — hide in a cupboard...

Try these Exam Practice Questions to have a go at rearranging more complicated formulas...

Q1 Make y the subject of: a) $x = \dfrac{y^2}{4}$ [2 marks] b) $x = \dfrac{y}{y - z}$ [3 marks]

Q2 The imperial formula for BMI, b, is $b = \dfrac{703w}{h^2}$ where w is weight in pounds and h is height in inches. Make h the subject. [3 marks]

Functions and Straight Line Graphs

The two topics on this page aren't really related... but I haven't just shoved them on the same page because I couldn't think of anywhere else to put them. Honest.

Function Notation Uses 'f(x) = ' Instead of 'y = '

A <u>function</u> takes an <u>input</u>, <u>processes</u> it and <u>outputs</u> a value. You write a function like this: <u>f(x) = 5x + 2</u>. This says 'the function f takes a value for x, <u>multiplies</u> it by <u>5</u> and <u>adds 2</u>.
Functions can look a bit scary-mathsy, but they're just like <u>equations</u> but with y replaced by <u>f(x)</u>.
<u>Evaluating</u> functions is easy — just pop the numbers into the function and you're away.

EXAMPLES:

1. $f(x) = 2x + 1$
Find the value of f(0).

Just swap all the x's with 0's. — $f(0) = 2(0) + 1 = 1$

2. $f(x) = x^2 - x + 7$. Find: a) f(3) and b) f(−2)

a) $f(3) = (3)^2 - (3) + 7 = 9 - 3 + 7 = 13$

b) $f(-2) = (-2)^2 - (-2) + 7 = 4 + 2 + 7 = 13$

3. Given that $f(x) = 3\sqrt{x}$ and $f(k) = 27$, find k.

If you get a question like this, rearrange the function to make k the subject. Check p.19-20 if you're unsure about rearranging.

$f(k) = 3\sqrt{k} = 27$
$\sqrt{k} = 27 \div 3 = 9$
$k = 9^2 = 81$

Learn to Spot These Straight Line Equations

If an equation has a y and/or x but <u>no higher powers</u> (like x^2 or x^3) then it's a <u>straight line</u> equation. Equations like this are called <u>linear</u> equations.

Vertical lines: 'x = a'

'<u>x = a</u>' is a <u>vertical line</u> <u>through 'a'</u> on the x-axis.

Horizontal lines: 'y = a'

'<u>y = a</u>' is a <u>horizontal line</u> <u>through 'a'</u> on the y-axis.

The equation of the <u>x-axis</u> is $y = 0$. The equation of the <u>y-axis</u> is $x = 0$.

The <u>main diagonal</u> through the <u>origin</u>: 'y = x'

'<u>y = x</u>' is the <u>main diagonal</u> that goes <u>UPHILL</u> from left to right and passes through the origin (0, 0).

$y = -x$ is the main diagonal sloping <u>downhill</u>.

Other <u>sloping lines</u> through the <u>origin</u>: 'y = ax'

The value of '<u>a</u>' is the <u>gradient</u> — see the next page.

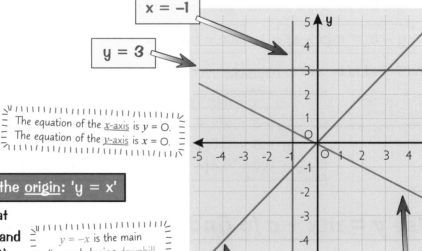

$x = -1$

$y = 3$

$y = x$

$y = -\frac{1}{2}x$

This page has really put the 'fun' into 'functions'...

Nothing dramatic on this page — just a look at function notation and an introduction to straight lines. Don't panic, there'll be more on those in a moment. In the meantime, try these beauties...

Q1   The function f(x) is defined by $f(x) = \dfrac{x^2}{\sqrt{x} - 2}$ for $x \geq 0$, $x \neq 4$. Evaluate f(9).   [2 marks]

Q2   On the same set of axes, sketch the graphs of $y = 5$, $x = 5$, $y = -5$ and $y = -x$.   [2 marks]

Straight Line Graphs

Time to hit the slopes. Well, spot them and work out their steepness anyway...

The Gradient is the Steepness of the Line

The <u>gradient</u> of the line is how <u>steep</u> it is — the <u>larger</u> the gradient, the <u>steeper</u> the slope.
A <u>negative gradient</u> tells you it slopes <u>downhill</u>. You find it by dividing the <u>change in y</u> by the <u>change in x</u>.

EXAMPLE: Find the gradient of the straight line going through points A and B below.

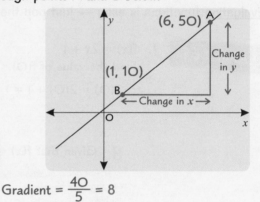

1 Find the <u>change in y</u> and <u>change in x</u>.

Change in y = 50 – 10 = 40
Change in x = 6 – 1 = 5

Make sure you subtract the y and x-coordinates in the
same order. E.g. $y_A - y_B$ and $x_A - x_B$

2 Use this <u>formula</u>:

$$\text{GRADIENT} = \frac{\text{CHANGE IN Y}}{\text{CHANGE IN X}}$$

Gradient = $\frac{40}{5}$ = 8

Always check the <u>sign</u> of your gradient.
Remember, uphill = <u>positive</u> and downhill = <u>negative</u>

If two lines have the <u>same gradient</u> then they're <u>parallel</u>.

All <u>horizontal lines</u> have a gradient of <u>0</u> (because the <u>change in y</u> is 0).

Straight Line Equations Come in Three Different Forms

Straight line equations are often given in one of three different forms:

$$y - b = m(x - a)$$ $$ax + by + c = 0$$ $$y = mx + c$$

m is the gradient and c is the y-intercept — see below.

You'll need to be able to <u>rearrange</u> your equation from one format to another:

In this form, a and b are the coordinates (a, b), which will be on the line.

<u>y – a = m(x – b)</u>		<u>y = mx +c</u>		<u>ax + by + c = 0</u>
$y - 3 = 2(x + 1)$	→	$y = 2x + 5$	→	$2x - y + 5 = 0$
$y + 8 = 0.5(x - 2)$	→	$y = 0.5x - 9$	→	$x - 2y - 18 = 0$
$y + 0.2 = 0.4(x + 3)$	→	$y = 0.4x + 1$	→	$2x - 5y + 5 = 0$

Use y = mx + c to find the Gradient and y-Intercept

You might be given the equation of a line in <u>any form</u> and asked to find the <u>gradient</u> and <u>y-intercept</u>
(where the line crosses the y-axis). <u>Rearrange</u> it into the form <u>y = mx + c</u> to be able to <u>read off</u>
these values straight from the equation — <u>m is the gradient</u> of the line and <u>c is the y-intercept</u>.

EXAMPLE: The equation $3x + 2y + 1 = 0$ describes a straight line.
Determine the gradient of the line and the coordinates
of the point where the line meets the y-axis.

1 Rearrange the equation
into the form y = mx + c.

$3x + 2y + 1 = 0$
$2y = -3x - 1$
$y = -\frac{3}{2}x - \frac{1}{2}$

2 Read off the gradient (m)
and the y-intercept (c).

Gradient = $m = -\frac{3}{2}$

y-intercept = $(0, c) = \left(0, -\frac{1}{2}\right)$

If you're asked for the coordinates, don't forget the x-coordinate too — it's 0.

Straight Line Graphs

Finding the Equation of a Line Through Two Points

If you're given two points, it's easiest to find the equation in the form $y - a = m(x - b)$ and then <u>change it</u> into the form the question is asking you for.

 **EXAMPLE:** Find the equation of the straight line that passes through $(-2, 9)$ and $(3, -1)$.
Give your answer in the form $y = mx + c$.

1 Use the <u>two</u> points to find 'm' (gradient).

$$m = \frac{\text{change in } y}{\text{change in } x} = \frac{-1 - 9}{3 - (-2)} = \frac{-10}{5} = -2$$

2 Use <u>one</u> of the points to write down the equation in the form $y - b = m(x - a)$.

$m = -2$, let $(a, b) = (-2, 9)$
So $y - 9 = -2(x - (-2))$

> You could have used the other point — you'd get the same answer.

3 <u>Rearrange</u> the equation into the form $y = mx + c$.

$y - 9 = -2(x + 2)$
$y - 9 = -2x - 4$
$y = -2x + 5$

Now celebrate the only way graphs know how: line dancing.

Finding the Equation of a Line Given the Gradient

The method is almost exactly the same if you're given <u>one point</u> and the <u>gradient</u> — but you don't need to bother with step 1.

 **EXAMPLE:** The graph on the right shows how degrees Celcius (°C) relate to degrees Fahrenheit (°F). A temperature of 20 °C is equivalent to 68 °F. An increase in temperature of 1 °C is equivalent to an increase of 1.8 °F.

Find the equation of the line in the form $y = mx + c$.

You know that the <u>point</u> $(a, b) = (20, 68)$ is on the line and that the <u>gradient</u> is $m = 1.8$ — so use the form $\underline{y - b = m(x - a)}$.

$y - 68 = 1.8(x - 20)$
$y = 1.8x - 36 + 68$
$y = 1.8x + 32$

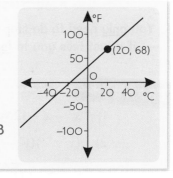

Finding gradients is often an uphill battle...

There's lots to take in on these pages but I have every faith in you. The different forms aren't really all that different — it just comes down to how they're factorised and arranged. One quick warning though: be careful with gradients. The two points you use might not have nice, positive coordinates.

Q1 Find the gradient of the line shown on the right. [1 mark]

Q2 a) Find the gradient of the straight line with equation $7x - 3y + 10 = 0$. [2 marks]

b) State the coordinates of the point where the line crosses the y-axis. [1 mark]

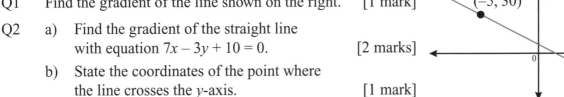

Q3 Line L goes through $(0, 1)$ and $(9, 16)$. Line M goes through $(21, 3)$ and $(9, -1)$.

a) Find the equation of Line L in the form $ax + by + c = 0$ (a, b and c integers). [3 marks]

b) Find the equation of Line M in the form $y = mx + c$. [3 marks]

Q4 A straight line has a gradient of -2. Given that the line passes through the point $(2, 5)$, determine the equation of the line in the form $ax + by + c = 0$. [2 marks]

Factorising Quadratics

<u>Quadratic equations</u> (equations with an $\underline{x^2}$ in them) can be solved in a number of <u>different ways</u>.
And you're about to find out all about them on the <u>next few pages</u>...

Factorising a Quadratic

1) '<u>Factorising a quadratic</u>' means '<u>putting it into 2 brackets</u>'.

2) The standard format for quadratic equations is: $\underline{ax^2 + bx + c = 0}$.

3) If <u>a = 1</u>, the quadratic is <u>much easier</u> to deal with. E.g. $x^2 + 3x + 2 = 0$ (You'll see what to do when $a \neq 1$ on the next page.)

4) As well as factorising a quadratic, you might be asked to <u>solve</u> the equation. This just means finding the values of x that make each bracket <u>0</u> (see example below).

> Expressions of the form $ax^2 + bx + c$ are called trinomials. They have 3 terms, hence the 'tri'.

Factorising Method when a = 1

1) <u>ALWAYS</u> rearrange into the <u>STANDARD FORMAT</u>: $x^2 + bx + c = 0$.

2) Write down the <u>TWO BRACKETS</u> with the x's in: $(x \quad)(x \quad) = 0$.

3) Then <u>find 2 numbers</u> that <u>MULTIPLY to give 'c'</u> (the end number) but also <u>ADD/SUBTRACT to give 'b'</u> (the coefficient of x).

> Ignore any minus signs at this stage.

4) Fill in the +/− signs and make sure they work out properly.

5) As an <u>ESSENTIAL CHECK</u>, <u>expand</u> the brackets to make sure they give the original equation.

6) Finally, <u>SOLVE THE EQUATION</u> by <u>setting each bracket equal to 0</u>.

> If the quadratic is already factorised, jump straight to step 6) — dead easy.

You <u>only</u> need to do step 6) if the question asks you to <u>solve</u> the equation — if it just tells you to <u>factorise</u>, you can <u>stop</u> at step 5).

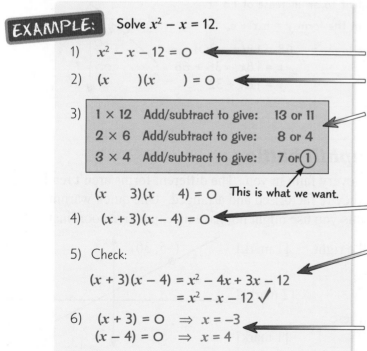

EXAMPLE: Solve $x^2 - x = 12$.

1) $x^2 - x - 12 = 0$

2) $(x \quad)(x \quad) = 0$

3)
1×12	Add/subtract to give:	13 or 11
2×6	Add/subtract to give:	8 or 4
3×4	Add/subtract to give:	7 or ①

$(x \quad 3)(x \quad 4) = 0$ This is what we want.

4) $(x + 3)(x - 4) = 0$

5) Check:

$(x + 3)(x - 4) = x^2 - 4x + 3x - 12$
$= x^2 - x - 12 \checkmark$

6) $(x + 3) = 0 \Rightarrow x = -3$
$(x - 4) = 0 \Rightarrow x = 4$

1) <u>Rearrange</u> into the standard format.

2) Write down the <u>initial brackets</u>.

3) Find the right <u>pairs of numbers</u> that <u>multiply to give c</u> (= 12), and <u>add or subtract to give b</u> (= 1) (remember, we're ignoring the +/− signs for now).

4) <u>Now fill in the +/− signs</u> so that 3 and 4 add/subtract to give −1 (= b).

5) <u>ESSENTIAL check</u> — <u>EXPAND the brackets</u> to make sure they give the original expression.

But we're not finished yet — we've only factorised it, we still need to...

6) <u>SOLVE THE EQUATION</u> by setting each bracket <u>equal to 0</u>.

Bring me a biscuit or I'll factorise your quadratic...

To help you work out which signs you need, look at c. If c is positive, the signs will be the same (both positive or negative), but if c is negative the signs will be different (one positive and one negative).

Q1   Factorise $x^2 + 2x - 15$ [1 mark]   Q2   Solve $x^2 - 9x + 20 = 0$ [2 marks]

Factorising Quadratics

So far so good. It gets a bit more complicated when a ≠ 1, but it's all good fun, right? Right?
Well, I think it's fun anyway.

When 'a' is Not 1

The basic method is still the same but it's <u>a bit messier</u> — the initial brackets are <u>different</u> as the first terms in each bracket have to multiply to give '<u>a</u>'. This means finding the <u>other</u> numbers to go in the brackets is harder as there are more <u>combinations</u> to try. The best way to get to grips with it is to look at an <u>example</u>.

EXAMPLE: Solve $3x^2 + 7x - 6 = 0$.

1) $3x^2 + 7x - 6 = 0$

2) $(3x\quad)(x\quad) = 0$

3) Number pairs: 1×6 and 2×3

> $(3x\quad 1)(x\quad 6)$ <u>multiplies</u> to give <u>18x and 1x</u> which <u>add/subtract</u> to give <u>17x or 19x</u>
>
> $(3x\quad 6)(x\quad 1)$ <u>multiplies</u> to give <u>3x and 6x</u> which <u>add/subtract</u> to give <u>9x or 3x</u>
>
> $(3x\quad 3)(x\quad 2)$ <u>multiplies</u> to give <u>6x and 3x</u> which <u>add/subtract</u> to give <u>9x or 3x</u>
>
> $(3x\quad 2)(x\quad 3)$ <u>multiplies</u> to give <u>9x and 2x</u> which <u>add/subtract</u> to give <u>11x or (7x)</u> ✓

$(3x\quad 2)(x\quad 3)$

4) $(3x - 2)(x + 3)$

5) $(3x - 2)(x + 3) = 3x^2 + 9x - 2x - 6$
$= 3x^2 + 7x - 6$ ✓

6) $(3x - 2) = 0 \Rightarrow x = \dfrac{2}{3}$
$(x + 3) = 0 \Rightarrow x = -3$

1) <u>Rearrange</u> into the standard format.

2) Write down the <u>initial brackets</u> — this time, one of the brackets will have a <u>3x</u> in it.

3) The <u>tricky part</u>: first, find <u>pairs of numbers</u> that <u>multiply to give c</u> (= 6), ignoring the minus sign for now.

Then, <u>try out</u> the number pairs you just found in the brackets until you find one that gives 7x. But remember, each pair of numbers has to be tried in <u>2 positions</u> (as the brackets are different — one has 3x in it).

4) <u>Now fill in the +/– signs</u> so that 9 and 2 add/subtract to give +7 (= b).

5) <u>ESSENTIAL check</u> — <u>EXPAND the brackets</u>.

6) <u>SOLVE THE EQUATION</u> by setting each bracket <u>equal to 0</u> (if a isn't 1, one of your answers will be a <u>fraction</u>).

EXAMPLE: Solve $2x^2 - 9x = 5$.

1) Put in standard form: $2x^2 - 9x - 5 = 0$

2) Initial brackets: $(2x\quad)(x\quad) = 0$

3) Number pairs: 1×5

> $(2x\quad 5)(x\quad 1)$ <u>multiplies</u> to give <u>2x and 5x</u> which <u>add/subtract</u> to give <u>3x or 7x</u>
>
> $(2x\quad 1)(x\quad 5)$ <u>multiplies</u> to give <u>1x and 10x</u> which <u>add/subtract</u> to give <u>(9x) or 11x</u>

$(2x\quad 1)(x\quad 5)$ ✓

4) Put in the signs: $(2x + 1)(x - 5)$

5) Check:
$(2x + 1)(x - 5) = 2x^2 - 10x + x - 5$
$= 2x^2 - 9x - 5$ ✓

6) Solve:
$(2x + 1) = 0 \Rightarrow x = -\dfrac{1}{2}$
$(x - 5) = 0 \Rightarrow x = 5$

It's not scary — just think of it as brackets giving algebra a hug...

Learn the step-by-step method above, then have a go at these nice practice questions.

Q1 Factorise $2x^2 - 5x - 12$ [2 marks] Q2 Solve $3x^2 + 10x - 8 = 0$ [3 marks]

Q3 Factorise $3x^2 + 32x + 20$ [2 marks] Q4 Solve $5x^2 - 13x = 6$ [3 marks]

The Quadratic Formula

The solutions to ANY quadratic equation $ax^2 + bx + c = 0$ are given by this formula:

$$x = \frac{-b \pm \sqrt{b^2 - 4ac}}{2a}$$

Don't fear — the quadratic formula is on the <u>formula sheet</u>. But you still need to learn <u>how to use it</u>. It isn't all that hard, but there are a few pitfalls — so <u>TAKE HEED of these crucial details</u>:

Quadratic Formula — Five Crucial Details

1) Take it nice and slowly — always write it down in stages as you go.

2) **WHENEVER YOU GET A MINUS SIGN, <u>THE ALARM BELLS SHOULD ALWAYS RING!</u>**

3) Remember it's '<u>2a</u>' on the bottom line, not just 'a' — and you <u>divide ALL of the top line by 2a</u>.

If either 'a' or 'c' is negative, the −4ac effectively becomes +4ac, so watch out. Also, be careful if b is negative, as −b will be positive.

4) The $\pm$ sign means you end up with <u>two solutions</u> (by replacing it in the final step with '+' and '−').

5) If you get a <u>negative</u> number inside your square root, go back and <u>check your working</u>. Some quadratics do have a negative value in the square root, but they won't come up at N5.

EXAMPLE: Solve $3x^2 + 7x = 1$, giving your answers to 2 decimal places.

$3x^2 + 7x - 1 = 0$

$a = 3, \quad b = 7, \quad c = -1$

$x = \dfrac{-b \pm \sqrt{b^2 - 4ac}}{2a}$

$= \dfrac{-7 \pm \sqrt{7^2 - 4 \times 3 \times -1}}{2 \times 3}$

$= \dfrac{-7 \pm \sqrt{49 + 12}}{6}$

$= \dfrac{-7 \pm \sqrt{61}}{6}$

$= \dfrac{-7 + \sqrt{61}}{6}$ or $\dfrac{-7 - \sqrt{61}}{6}$

$= 0.1350...$ or $-2.468...$

So to 2 d.p. the solutions are:
$x = 0.14$ or -2.47

Notice that you do two calculations at the final stage — one + and one −.

1) First get it into the form $\underline{ax^2 + bx + c = 0}$.

2) Then carefully identify a, b and c.

3) Put these values into the quadratic formula and <u>write down each stage</u>.

4) Finally, <u>as a check</u> put these values back into the <u>original equation</u>:
E.g. for x = 0.1350...:
$3 \times 0.135...^2 + 7 \times 0.135... = 1$

When to use the quadratic formula:

- If you have a quadratic that <u>won't</u> easily <u>factorise</u>.

- If the question mentions <u>decimal places</u> or <u>significant figures</u>.

- If the question asks for <u>exact answers</u> or <u>surds</u> (though this could be completing the square instead — see next page).

Enough number crunches? Now it's time to work on your quads...

You might have to do a bit of fancy rearranging to get your quadratic into the form $ax^2 + bx + c$.
In Q2 below, it doesn't even look like a quadratic until you start rearranging it and get rid of the fraction.

Q1   Solve $x^2 + 10x - 4 = 0$, giving your answers to 2 decimal places.   [3 marks]

Q2   Find the exact solutions of $2x + \dfrac{3}{x - 2} = -2$.   [4 marks]

Completing the Square

There's just one more method to learn for solving quadratics — and it's a bit of a nasty one.
It's called 'completing the square', and takes a bit to get your head round it.

Solving Quadratics by 'Completing the Square'

To 'complete the square' you have to:

1) Write down a <u>SQUARED</u> bracket, and then

2) Stick a number on the end to '<u>COMPLETE</u>' it.

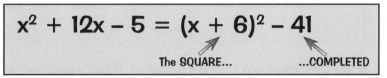

$$x^2 + 12x - 5 = (x + 6)^2 - 41$$

The SQUARE...   ...COMPLETED

It's not that bad if you <u>learn all the steps</u> — some of them aren't all that obvious.

1) As always, <u>REARRANGE THE QUADRATIC INTO THE STANDARD FORMAT</u>: $x^2 + bx + c$

2) <u>WRITE OUT THE INITIAL BRACKET</u>: $\left(x + \dfrac{b}{2}\right)^2$ — just divide the value of b by 2.

3) <u>MULTIPLY OUT THE BRACKETS</u> and <u>COMPARE TO THE ORIGINAL</u>
   to find what you need to add or subtract to complete the square.

4) Add or subtract the <u>ADJUSTING NUMBER</u> to make it <u>MATCH THE ORIGINAL</u>.

EXAMPLE: a) Express $x^2 + 8x + 5$ in the form $(x + m)^2 + n$.

1) It's in the <u>standard format</u>. —— $x^2 + 8x + 5$

2) Write out the <u>initial bracket</u> —— $(x + 4)^2$

   Original equation had $+5$ here...

3) Multiply out the brackets
   and <u>compare</u> to the original. $(x + 4)^2 = x^2 + 8x + 16$

   ...so you need -11

4) Subtract <u>adjusting number</u> (11). $(x + 4)^2 - 11 = x^2 + 8x + 16 - 11$

   $= x^2 + 8x + 5 \checkmark$ —— matches original now!

So the completed square is: $(x + 4)^2 - 11$

Now <u>use</u> the completed square
to solve the equation. There are
<u>three more steps</u> for this:

b) Hence solve $x^2 + 8x + 5 = 0$,
   leaving your answers in surd form.

$$(x + 4)^2 - 11 = 0$$

1) Put the number on the
   other side ($+11$).

$$(x + 4)^2 = 11$$

2) Square root both sides
   (don't forget the $\pm$!) ($\sqrt{\ }$).

$$x + 4 = \pm\sqrt{11}$$

3) Get x on its own (-4).

$$x = -4 \pm \sqrt{11}$$

So the two solutions (in surd form) are:
$x = -4 + \sqrt{11}$ and $x = -4 - \sqrt{11}$

If you really don't like steps 3-4, just remember that the value you need to add or subtract is <u>always</u> $c - \left(\dfrac{b}{2}\right)^2$.

But if a square's not complete, is it really a square...?

Go over this carefully, 'cos it's pretty darn confusing at first, then try these Exam Practice Questions.

Q1   Write $x^2 - 12x + 23$ in the form $(x + p)^2 + q$.   [2 marks]

Q2   Solve $x^2 + 10x + 7 = 0$ by first writing it in the form $(x + m)^2 + n = 0$.
     Give your answers as simplified surds.   [4 marks]

Quadratic Graphs

Graphs of quadratics all have the same <u>symmetrical</u> bucket shape — they're either u-shaped or n-shaped.

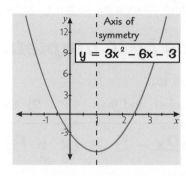

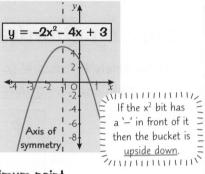

$y = x^2$

$y = 3x^2 - 6x - 3$

Axis of symmetry

$y = -2x^2 - 4x + 3$

This shape is known as a <u>parabola</u>.

Axis of symmetry

If the x^2 bit has a '−' in front of it then the bucket is <u>upside down</u>.

If the graph is <u>u-shaped</u>, it has a <u>minimum</u> point. If it's <u>n-shaped</u>, it has a <u>maximum</u> point.
These are known as <u>turning points</u> — the <u>nature</u> of the turning point is whether it's a minimum or a maximum.

If $y = kx^2$, the Graph is Symmetric About the y-Axis

All quadratics of the form $y = kx^2$ have the <u>same</u> axis of <u>symmetry</u> (the <u>y-axis</u>) and turning point <u>(0, 0)</u>.
The k just <u>stretches</u> the graph <u>vertically</u> (and <u>reflects</u> it in the x-axis if $k < 0$).

EXAMPLE: The diagram on the right shows part of the graph of $y = kx^2$. Find the value of k.

Put the <u>known values</u> of x and y into the equation of the curve and then <u>rearrange</u> to find k.

$y = kx^2$
$-20 = k \times 2^2$
$-20 = 4k$
So $k = -20 \div 4 = -5$

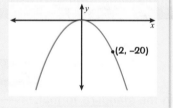

(2, −20)

Complete the Square to Find Symmetry and Turning Points

Other quadratic graphs will have the <u>same general shape</u> but will have a <u>different axis of symmetry</u> and <u>turning point</u>. You can find this information from the <u>completed square form</u> $k(x + p)^2 + q$:

1) The <u>axis of symmetry</u> is $x = -p$.

2) The <u>turning point</u> of the graph is at $y = q$. The x-coordinate is $x = -p$.

The turning point lies on the axis of symmetry, which is why the x-coordinate is $-p$.

EXAMPLE: The graph of $y = (x + a)^2 + b$ is shown below.
The axis of symmetry is $x = -6$.
Find the values of a and b, and the coordinates of the turning point.

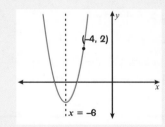

(−4, 2)

$x = -6$

The axis of symmetry is $x = -6 \Rightarrow -6 = -a$, so $a = 6$.
Use the given point to find b: $2 = (-4 + 6)^2 + b$
$2 = 2^2 + b$
$2 = 4 + b$
$b = -2$

So the turning point is $(-a, b) = (-6, -2)$.

Complete the following square: ☐

Who knew a little equation could tell you so much? Now have a go at this question...

Q1 The diagram to the right shows part of the graph of $y = k(x + p)^2 - 2$.

a) Given the parabola is symmetric about $x = 5$, find the value of p. [1 mark]

b) Given that the point (6, 5) lies on the parabola, find the value k. [2 marks]

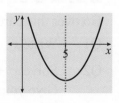

Sketching Quadratics

If you're asked to <u>sketch</u> a graph, you won't have to use <u>graph paper</u> or be dead <u>accurate</u> — just find and <u>label</u> the <u>important points</u> and make sure the graph is roughly in the <u>correct position</u> on the axes.

Factorise Quadratics to Find the Intercepts

Getting a quadratic in <u>factorised</u> form makes <u>sketching</u> it really simple.
You can see straight away where it crosses the <u>x-axis</u> and <u>y-axis</u>.

 **EXAMPLE:** Sketch the graph of $y = -x^2 - 2x + 8$, labelling the intercepts with the x- and y-axes and the turning point.

The <u>solutions</u> of the equation are the x-values of the points where the graph <u>crosses</u> the x-axis. These are also called the <u>roots</u> of the quadratic.

1 Find all the information you're asked for.

<u>Factorise</u> $-x^2 - 2x + 8 = 0$ to find the x-intercepts (see p.24-25):
$$-x^2 - 2x + 8 = -(x + 4)(x - 2) = 0 \text{ so } x = -4 \text{ and } x = 2$$

<u>Set $x = 0$</u> to find the y-intercepts:
$$y = -0^2 - 2 \times 0 + 8 = 8$$

The <u>y-intercept</u> is the value of $\underline{c}$ when the quadratic is written as $ax^2 + bx + \underline{c}$.

Use <u>symmetry</u> to find the turning point of the curve:

The x-coordinate of the turning point is <u>halfway between</u> the x-intercepts, so halfway between -4 and 2.
$$x = \frac{-4 + 2}{2} = -1$$
$$y = -(-1)^2 - 2(-1) + 8 = 9$$
So the turning point is $(-1, 9)$.

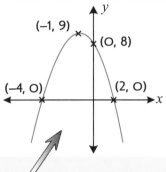

2 Use the information you know to sketch the curve and label the important points.

The x^2 coefficient (-1) is <u>negative</u>, so the curve is <u>n-shaped</u>.
It will be <u>symmetric</u> about $x = -1$.

The Completed Square Helps You Sketch the Graph

You saw on the previous page how the <u>completed square</u> form helps you find the axis of <u>symmetry</u> and the <u>turning point</u>. You can use this information to help you <u>sketch</u> the graph as well.

1) If the completed square is $k(x + p)^2 + q$, the turning point is <u>$(-p, q)$</u> and the axis of symmetry is <u>$x = -p$</u>.

2) The <u>solutions</u> to the equation tell you where the graph <u>crosses</u> the <u>x-axis</u>. However, if <u>q is positive</u>, the graph will <u>never</u> cross the x-axis as it will always be greater than 0 (the brackets are squared so can <u>never</u> be less than 0). This means that the quadratic has <u>no real roots</u> — see next page.

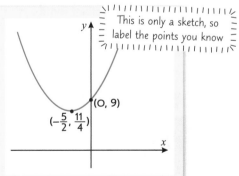

EXAMPLE: Sketch the graph of $y = x^2 + 5x + 9$.

The <u>completed square form</u> is $\left(x + \frac{5}{2}\right)^2 + \frac{11}{4}$.

The <u>minimum point</u> occurs at $\left(-\frac{5}{2}, \frac{11}{4}\right)$.

Since the adjusting number $\frac{11}{4}$ is <u>positive</u>, the graph will <u>never</u> cross the x-axis.

Find where the curve crosses the y-axis by substituting $x = 0$ into the equation and mark this on your graph. $y = 0 + 0 + 9 = 9$

This is only a sketch, so label the points you know

A bit of hard grapht never hurt anyone — get revising...

Fun fact* — you could have also found the turning point in the first example by completing the square.

Q1 Sketch the graph of $y = x^2 + x - 6$ showing any points of intersection with the axes. [3 marks]

Q2 Sketch the graph of $y = (x - 2)^2 - 5$, indicating the coordinates of the turning point and the point of intersection with the y-axis. [3 marks]

*fun not guaranteed.

Section Two — Algebraic Skills

The Discriminant

Remember the quadratic formula — you bumped into it on page 26. Well, it tells you more than you think...

The Discriminant is Inside the Square Root

$$x = \frac{-b \pm \sqrt{b^2 - 4ac}}{2a}$$

When you use the <u>quadratic formula</u>, the bit inside the square root sign ($b^2 - 4ac$) is called the <u>discriminant</u>.

EXAMPLES:

1. Find the discriminant of $3x^2 + 2x + 1$.

$a = 3$, $b = 2$, $c = 1$

So the discriminant is $b^2 - 4ac = 2^2 - (4 \times 3 \times 1)$
$$= 4 - 12$$
$$= -8$$

2. Find the discriminant of $15 - x - 2x^2$.

$a = -2$, $b = -1$ and $c = 15$
(NOT $a = 15$, $b = -1$ and $c = -2$)
$$b^2 - 4ac = (-1)^2 - (4 \times -2 \times 15)$$
$$= 1 + 120 = 121$$

The discriminant can be <u>positive</u>, <u>negative</u> or <u>zero</u> — and this tells you <u>how many roots</u> the quadratic has.

How Many Roots? Check the Discriminant...

$b^2 - 4ac > 0$	$b^2 - 4ac = 0$	$b^2 - 4ac < 0$
Two real, distinct roots	One real, repeated root (or two equal real roots)	No real roots

The graph <u>crosses</u> the x-axis <u>twice</u> and these values are the roots.

$\underline{y = x^2 - 6x + 8}$:
$b^2 - 4ac = (-6)^2 - (4 \times 1 \times 8)$
$$= 36 - 32 = 4 > 0$$

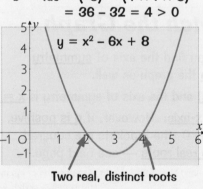

Two real, distinct roots

The graph just <u>touches</u> the x-axis from above (or from below if the x^2 coefficient is negative).

$\underline{y = x^2 - 6x + 9}$:
$b^2 - 4ac = (-6)^2 - (4 \times 1 \times 9)$
$$= 36 - 36 = 0$$

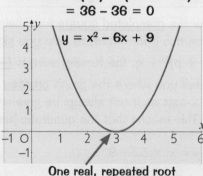

One real, repeated root

The graph <u>doesn't</u> touch or cross the x-axis <u>at all</u>.

$\underline{y = x^2 - 6x + 10}$:
$b^2 - 4ac = (-6)^2 - (4 \times 1 \times 10)$
$$= 36 - 40 = -4 < 0$$

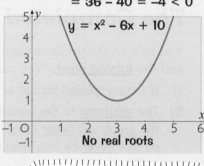

No real roots

Real roots are where a graph crosses the x-axis. Functions can have imaginary roots, but you don't have to worry about them for N5.

EXAMPLE: Determine the nature of the roots of the function $f(x) = 4x^2 - 36x + 81$.

Write down a, b and c. —— $a = 4$, $b = -36$, $c = 81$

Find the discriminant. —— $b^2 - 4ac = (-36)^2 - (4 \times 4 \times 81)$
$$= 1296 - 1296 = 0$$

Work out what this tells you about the number of roots. So $f(x)$ has one real, repeated root.

This is just asking you to work out <u>how many</u> roots a function has and what <u>type</u> they are.

All the best mathematicians are raised on a quadratic formula...

Always use the proper language when talking about roots in the exam — distinct, repeated, real, etc...

Q1 Find the discriminant of the following functions and determine the nature of their roots.

a) $4x^2 + 28x + 49 = 0$ [2 marks] b) $3x^2 + 3x + 1 = 0$ [2 marks] c) $2x^2 + 9x - 5 = 0$ [2 marks]

Algebraic Fractions

Unfortunately, fractions aren't limited to numbers — you can get <u>algebraic fractions</u> too.
Fortunately, everything you learnt about fractions on p.2-3 can be applied to algebraic fractions as well.

Simplifying Algebraic Fractions

You can <u>simplify</u> algebraic fractions by <u>cancelling</u> terms on the top and bottom — just deal with each <u>letter</u> individually and cancel as much as you can. You might have to <u>factorise</u> first (see pages 15 and 24-25).

EXAMPLES:

1. Simplify $\dfrac{21x^3y^2}{14xy^3}$

÷7 on the top and bottom

÷x on the top and bottom
to leave x^2 on the top

÷y^2 on the top and bottom
to leave y on the bottom

$$\dfrac{\overset{3}{\cancel{21}}x^3\overset{x^2}{\cancel{y^2}}}{\underset{2}{\cancel{14}}x\underset{y}{\cancel{y^3}}} = \dfrac{3x^2}{2y}$$

2. Simplify $\dfrac{x^2-16}{x^2+2x-8}$

Factorise the top
using D.O.T.S.

$$\dfrac{(x+4)(x-4)}{(x-2)(x+4)} = \dfrac{x-4}{x-2}$$

Factorise the quadratic
on the bottom

Then cancel the common
factor of $(x + 4)$

Multiplying/Dividing Algebraic Fractions

1) To <u>multiply</u> two fractions, just multiply tops and bottoms <u>separately</u>.
2) To <u>divide</u>, turn the second fraction <u>upside down</u> then <u>multiply</u>.

EXAMPLE: Simplify $\dfrac{x^2-4}{x^2+x-12} \div \dfrac{2x+4}{x^2-3x}$

Turn the second fraction upside down   Factorise and cancel   Multiply tops and bottoms

$$\dfrac{x^2-4}{x^2+x-12} \div \dfrac{2x+4}{x^2-3x} = \dfrac{x^2-4}{x^2+x-12} \times \dfrac{x^2-3x}{2x+4} = \dfrac{(x+2)(x-2)}{(x+4)(x-3)} \times \dfrac{x(x-3)}{2(x+2)} = \dfrac{x-2}{x+4} \times \dfrac{x}{2} = \dfrac{x(x-2)}{2(x+4)}$$

Adding/Subtracting Algebraic Fractions

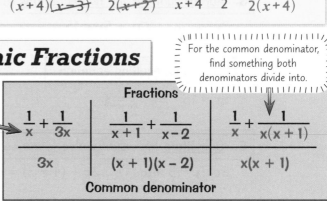

For the common denominator,
find something both
denominators divide into.

<u>Adding</u> or <u>subtracting</u> is a bit more difficult:

1) Work out the <u>common denominator</u> (see p.3).
2) Multiply <u>top and bottom</u> of each fraction by whatever gives you the common denominator.
3) Add or subtract the <u>numerators</u> only.

Fractions		
$\dfrac{1}{x} + \dfrac{1}{3x}$	$\dfrac{1}{x+1} + \dfrac{1}{x-2}$	$\dfrac{1}{x} + \dfrac{1}{x(x+1)}$
$3x$	$(x+1)(x-2)$	$x(x+1)$

Common denominator

EXAMPLE: Write $\dfrac{3}{(x+3)} + \dfrac{1}{(x-2)}$ as a single fraction.

1st fraction: × top & bottom by $(x - 2)$
2nd fraction: × top & bottom by $(x + 3)$

$$\dfrac{3}{(x+3)} + \dfrac{1}{(x-2)} = \dfrac{3(x-2)}{(x+3)(x-2)} + \dfrac{(x+3)}{(x+3)(x-2)}$$

Common denominator
will be $(x + 3)(x - 2)$

Add the numerators

$$= \dfrac{3x-6}{(x+3)(x-2)} + \dfrac{x+3}{(x+3)(x-2)} = \dfrac{4x-3}{(x+3)(x-2)}$$

I'd like to cancel the Autumn Term...

One more thing... never do this: $\dfrac{\cancel{x}}{\cancel{x}+y} = \dfrac{1}{y}$ ✗ It's wrong wrong WRONG! Got that? Sure? Good.

Q1   Simplify $\dfrac{x^4-4y^2}{x^3-2xy}$ [3 marks]

Q2   Simplify $\dfrac{y^2}{9(x-2)} \div \dfrac{y}{6x-12}$ [3 marks]

Q3   Write $\dfrac{2}{x+5} + \dfrac{3}{x-2}$ as a single fraction in its simplest form.   [3 marks]

Simultaneous Equations

If you have <u>two equations</u> in terms of <u>two unknowns</u> like x and y (e.g. $2x + y = 4$, $x + 5y = 9$) and you're asked to solve them <u>simultaneously</u>, you need to find the values of x and y that satisfy both equations at the <u>same time</u>. Read on to discover all...

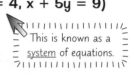

This is known as a <u>system</u> of equations.

Six Steps for Easy Simultaneous Equations

Follow these <u>six steps</u> for sure-fire <u>simultaneous equation success</u>...

EXAMPLE: Solve the simultaneous equations $2x = 6 - 4y$ and $-3 - 3y = 4x$

1. <u>Rearrange both equations</u> into the form <u>$ax + by = c$</u>, and label the two equations ① and ②.

$$2x + 4y = 6 \quad — \quad ①$$
$$4x + 3y = -3 \quad — \quad ②$$

a, b and c are numbers (which can be negative)

2. <u>Match up the numbers in front</u> (the 'coefficients') of either the x's or y's in both equations. You may need to multiply one or both equations by a suitable number. Relabel them ③ and ④.

$$① \times 2: \quad 4x + 8y = 12 \quad — \quad ③$$
$$4x + 3y = -3 \quad — \quad ④$$

3. <u>Add or subtract the two equations</u> to eliminate the terms with the same coefficient.

$$③ - ④ \quad 0x + 5y = 15$$

If the coefficients have the same sign (both +ve or both −ve) then subtract. If the coefficients have opposite signs (one +ve and one −ve) then add.

4. <u>Solve</u> the resulting equation.

$$5y = 15 \quad \Rightarrow \quad \underline{y = 3}$$

5. <u>Substitute</u> the value you've found back into equation ① and <u>solve</u> it.

Sub $y = 3$ into ①: $\quad 2x + (4 \times 3) = 6 \quad \Rightarrow \quad 2x + 12 = 6 \quad \Rightarrow \quad 2x = -6 \quad \Rightarrow \quad \underline{x = -3}$

6. <u>Substitute</u> both these values into equation ② to <u>make sure it works</u>. If it doesn't then you've done something <u>wrong</u> and you'll have to do it all again.

Sub x and y into ②: $\quad (4 \times -3) + (3 \times 3) = -12 + 9 = -3$, which is right, so it's worked.

So the solutions are: $\quad x = -3, \quad y = 3$

Make sure you've got your head round this method — things get a bit more involved on the next page, so you need to be completely happy with it.

Sunday morning, lemon squeezy & simultaneous equations...

You need to learn all 6 steps on this page — when you've found x and y, don't forget to do step 6 and check that they're actually right. Once you're okay with them, try out these Exam Practice Questions.

Q1   Find x and y given that $2x - 10 = 4y$ and $3y = 5x - 18$.   [3 marks]

Q2   Solve algebraically the system of equations $10x + 9y = 35$, $6x - 3y = 7$.   [3 marks]

Simultaneous Equations

Simultaneous equations aren't always laid out for you on a platter.
Sometimes you'll need to set them up for yourself...

Simultaneous Equations Can Be Hidden in Words

In some questions, you might have to <u>set up your own</u> simultaneous equations using <u>information</u> given in the <u>question</u> before you can solve them.

EXAMPLE: On one summer day, the earnings of an ice cream van were £170.85. 57 tubs of ice cream and 102 cones of ice cream were sold that day.

One day in winter, the earnings of the ice cream van were £12.15. 3 tubs of ice cream and 8 cones of ice cream were sold that day.

Calculate the cost of a tub and the cost of a cone of ice cream.

Work out what is wanted and write in terms of variables. — Let t = cost of a tub and c = cost of a cone.

Set up simultaneous equations using the information in the question.

Summer day: $57t + 102c = 170.85$ — ①
Winter day: $3t + 8c = 12.15$ — ②

> The exam question might ask you for each equation <u>separately</u> and then ask you to solve them simultaneously.

Solve the simultaneous equations. —

② × 19: $57t + 152c = 230.85$ — ③
③ − ① $0t + 50c = 60$
$c = 1.2$

Substitute into ②:
$3t + (8 × 1.2) = 12.15 \Rightarrow 3t + 9.6 = 12.15 \Rightarrow 3t = 2.55 \Rightarrow t = 0.85$

Check by substituting t and c into ①:
$(57 × 0.85) + (102 × 1.2) = 48.45 + 122.4 = 170.85$ ✓

Remember to give the answer in the context of the question. — The cost of a tub is 85p and the cost of a cone is £1.20.

Solutions Correspond to Points of Intersection

The solution of a pair of simultaneous equations is actually where the <u>graphs</u> of the two equations <u>intersect</u>. To find the <u>point of intersection</u>, <u>solve</u> the system of equations.

EXAMPLE: Find the points of intersection of the graphs of $y = 2x + 4$ and $y = -1 - 3x$, shown below.

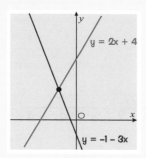

$y = 2x + 4$
$y = -1 - 3x$

Solve the simultaneous equations to find the point of intersection:

$2x - y = -4$ — ①
$3x + y = -1$ — ②

① + ② $5x + 0y = -5$
$x = -1$

Substituting x into ①: $(2 × -1) - y = -4 \Rightarrow -2 - y = -4 \Rightarrow y = 2$
Subtituting x and y into ② to check: $(3 × -1) + 2 = -3 + 2 = -1$ ✓
So the point of intersection is $(-1, 2)$.

Yes, I'm paying attention — I can simultaneously listen and text...

If you're answering a wordy question, always give your final answer in the context of the question. There might be an extra mark up for grabs if you do, so make sure you don't go and throw it away.

Q1 The equations below describe straight lines. Find the points of intersection between the lines.
 a) $y = 2x - 3$ and $y = 6 - x$ [2 marks] b) $x + 5y = 25$ and $y = 2x + 5$ [3 marks]

Revision Questions for Section Two

There's no denying, Section Two is grisly grimsdike algebra — so check now how much you've learned.
- Try these questions and tick off each one when you get it right.
- When you've done all the questions for a topic and are completely happy with it, tick off the topic.

Expanding Brackets and Factorising (p13-15)

1) Multiply out these brackets: a) $3(2x + 1)$ b) $(x + 2)(x – 3)$ c) $(x + 3)(x + 5)$

2) Expand the following: a) $(7x – 1)(2x^2 + 10x – 1)$ b) $5(5x + 7) + 2(7x + 2)$

3) Factorise: a) $8x – 2xy^2$ b) $49 – 81p^2q^2$ c) $12x^2 – 48y^2$

Solving Equations, Inequalities and Rearranging Formulas (p16-20)

4) Solve these equations: a) $5(x + 2) = 8 + 4(5 – x)$ b) $\dfrac{9x - 2}{2} = \dfrac{3x + 1}{9}$

5) Solve the following inequalities: a) $4x + 3 \leq 6x + 7$ b) $\dfrac{x}{5} + 9 > -20$

6) Make p the subject of these: a) $\dfrac{p}{p + y} = 4$ b) $\dfrac{1}{p} = \dfrac{1}{q} + \dfrac{1}{r}$

Straight Line Graphs (p21-23)

7) Find the gradient and y-intercept of the lines:
   a) $5x + 2y = 1$ b) $-y + 1 = 3x – 9$ c) $3x = 2y$

8) Find the equation of the line passing through $(3, –6)$ and $(6, –3)$ in the form $y = mx + c$.

9) Find the equation of the line passing through $(1, 9)$ with gradient $–3$ in the form $y = mx + c$.

Quadratics (p24-30)

10) Solve the following by factorising them first: a) $x^2 + 9x + 18 = 0$ b) $5x^2 – 17x – 12 = 0$

11) Find the solutions of these equations (to 2 d.p.) using the quadratic formula:
    a) $x^2 + x – 4 = 0$ b) $5x^2 + 6x = 2$ c) $(2x + 3)^2 = 15$

12) Find the exact solutions of these equations by completing the square:
    a) $x^2 + 12x + 15 = 0$ b) $x^2 – 6x = 2$

13) The point $(5, 10)$ lies on the curve $y = kx^2$. What is the value of k?

14) The graph of a quadratic function has a minimum turning point at $(2, 5)$.
    Write the quadratic as $(x – p)^2 + q$.

15) Sketch the graphs of the following. Label any known points.
    a) $y = (x + 2)(x – 2)$ b) $y = (x + 3)^2 – 37$

16) Describe the nature of the roots of a quadratic with discriminant:
    a) zero,   b) greater than zero,   c) less than zero.

Algebraic Fractions (p31)

17) Simplify: a) $\dfrac{25xyz}{10x^2z^3}$ b) $\dfrac{4x^2 - y^2}{(2x - y)^2}$ c) $\dfrac{3x}{x - y} \times \dfrac{4y}{(x - y)^2}$ d) $\dfrac{12x}{x + 2} \div \dfrac{3}{x^2 + 4x + 4}$

18) Write $\dfrac{2}{x + 3} + \dfrac{1}{x - 1}$ as a single fraction.

Simultaneous Equations (p32-33)

19) Solve the following pair of simultaneous equations: $4x + 5y = 23$ and $3y – x = 7$.

20) Find algebraically the point of intersection of the lines $4y – 2x = 32$ and $2y – 12 = 3x$.

21) a) Issy buys two cups of tea and three slices of cake for £9. Write down an equation to show this.
    b) Rudy buys four cups of tea and one slice of cake for £8. Write down an equation to show this.
    c) Hence find the cost of one cup of tea and the cost of one slice of cake.

Geometry

Think of this page as Geometry 101 — you need to know these basics about angles, triangles and quadrilaterals before moving on to the more complicated stuff coming up...

Angles *in Triangles* and *Quadrilaterals*

Angles in a <u>triangle</u> add up to 180°.

EQUILATERAL

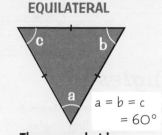

$a = b = c$
$= 60°$

Three equal sides
Three equal 60° angles

ISOSCELES

$a = b$

Two equal sides
Two equal angles

RIGHT-ANGLED

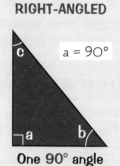

$a = 90°$

One 90° angle

SCALENE

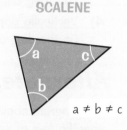

$a \neq b \neq c$

Three unequal sides
Three unequal angles

EXAMPLE: Find the size of angle x.

$180° - 40° = 140°$
<u>The two angles on the right are the same</u> (they're both x) and
they must add up to 140°, so $2x = 140°$, which means $x = 70°$.

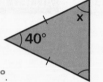

In an isosceles triangle, you only need to know <u>one angle</u> to be able to find the other two.

Angles in a <u>quadrilateral</u> add up to 360°.

TRAPEZIUM

One pair of parallel sides

PARALLELOGRAM

$a = c$
$b = d$

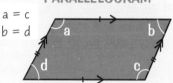

Two pairs of equal sides
Two pairs of parallel sides
Two pairs of equal angles

RHOMBUS

$a = c$
$b = d$

Four equal sides
Two pairs of parallel sides
Two pairs of equal angles

KITE

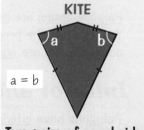

$a = b$

Two pairs of equal sides
One pair of equal angles

Angles *on Lines* and *Around Points*

Angles on a <u>straight line</u> add up to 180°.

$a + b + c = 180°$

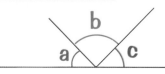

Angles <u>round a point</u> add up to 360°.

$a + b + c + d = 360°$

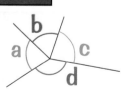

Heaven must be missing an angle...

All the basic facts are pretty easy really, but they could be hidden within more complicated questions. Have a go at this one as a bit of a warm-up:

Q1 Find the size of the angle marked x. [2 marks]

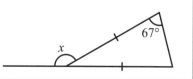

Geometry

There are a few more <u>rules</u> you need to learn here — make sure you don't get them mixed up.

Angles Around Parallel Lines

1) When a line crosses two <u>parallel lines</u>, it forms special sets of angles.

2) The two <u>bunches</u> of angles formed at the points of intersection <u>are the same</u>.

3) There are only actually <u>two different angles</u> involved (labelled a and b here), and they add up to <u>180°</u> (since they're <u>angles on a line</u>).

4) <u>Vertically opposite angles</u> (ones opposite each other) are <u>equal</u> (in the diagram, the a's are vertically opposite, as are the b's).

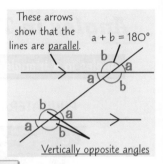

These arrows show that the lines are <u>parallel</u>.

a + b = 180°

<u>Vertically opposite angles</u>

Alternate, Allied and Corresponding Angles

The diagram above has some <u>characteristic shapes</u> to look out for — and each shape contains a specific <u>pair of angles</u>. The angle pairs are known as <u>alternate</u>, <u>allied</u> and <u>corresponding angles</u>.

Look out for the <u>characteristic Z, C, U and F shapes</u>:

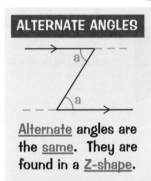

ALTERNATE ANGLES

<u>Alternate</u> angles are the <u>same</u>. They are found in a <u>Z-shape</u>.

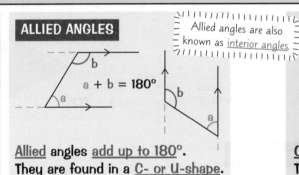

ALLIED ANGLES

Allied angles are also known as <u>interior angles</u>.

a + b = 180°

<u>Allied</u> angles <u>add up to 180°</u>. They are found in a <u>C- or U-shape</u>.

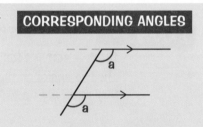

CORRESPONDING ANGLES

<u>Corresponding</u> angles are the <u>same</u>. They are found in an <u>F-shape</u>.

<u>Parallelograms</u> are <u>quadrilaterals</u> made from <u>two sets</u> of <u>parallel lines</u>. You can use the properties above to show that <u>opposite angles</u> in a parallelogram are <u>equal</u>, and each pair of <u>neighbouring angles</u> add up to <u>180°</u>.

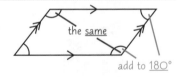

the <u>same</u>

add to <u>180°</u>

Interior and Exterior Angles

Polygons have <u>interior</u> and <u>exterior angles</u> — you need to know <u>what</u> they are and <u>how to find them</u>. There are a couple of <u>formulas</u> you need to learn as well.

For <u>ANY POLYGON</u> (regular or irregular):

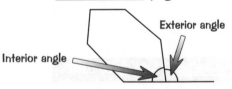

Exterior angle

Interior angle

SUM OF EXTERIOR ANGLES = 360°

SUM OF INTERIOR ANGLES = (n − 2) × 180°

(n is the number of sides)

This is because a polygon can be divided up into (n − 2) triangles, and the sum of angles in a triangle is 180°.

For <u>REGULAR POLYGONS</u> only:

EXTERIOR ANGLE $= \dfrac{360°}{n}$

INTERIOR ANGLE = 180° − EXTERIOR ANGLE

Exterior angles

Each sector triangle is <u>ISOSCELES</u>.

Interior angles

This angle is <u>always</u> the same as the <u>exterior angles</u>.

Aim for a gold medal in the parallel lines...

Lots to remember here — and make sure you know the proper names for all these angles as well.

Q1 The diagram shows two overlapping, identical regular pentagons. The angle ABC is 108°. Find the size of the angle DFE. [3 marks]

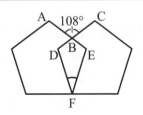

Geometry Problems

My biggest geometry problem is that I have to do geometry problems in the first place. *Sigh*
Ah well, best get practising — these problems aren't going to solve themselves.

Try Out All The Rules One By One

Don't concentrate too much on the angle you have been asked to find.
The best method is to find **ALL** the angles in whatever order they become obvious.

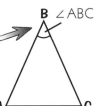

Before we get going, make sure you're familiar with three-letter angle notation, e.g. ∠ABC.
∠ABC, ABC and A$\hat{B}$C all mean 'the angle formed at **B**' (it's always the middle letter).
You might even see it written as just $\hat{B}$.

EXAMPLE: Find the size of angles x and y.

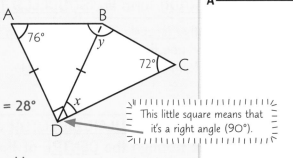

Write down everything you know
(or can work out) about the shape:

Triangle ABD is isosceles,
so ∠BAD = ∠ABD = 76°.
That means ∠ADB = 180° − 76° − 76° = 28°
∠ADC is a right angle (= 90°),
so angle x = 90° − 28° = 62°

This little square means that it's a right angle (90°).

ABCD is a quadrilateral, so all the angles add
up to 360°. 76° + 90° + y + 72° = 360°,
so y = 360° − 76° − 90° − 72° = 122°

You could have worked out angle y before angle x.

EXAMPLE: In the diagram below, BDF is a straight line. Find the size of angle BCD.

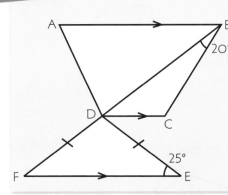

1) Triangle DEF is isosceles, so...
    ∠DFE = ∠DEF = 25°

2) FE and AB are parallel, so...
    ∠DFE and ∠ABD are
    alternate angles.
    So ∠ABD = ∠DFE = 25°

3) ∠ABC = ∠ABD + ∠CBD = 25° + 20° = 45°

4) DC and AB are parallel, so...
    ∠BCD and ∠ABC are allied angles.
    Allied angles add up to 180°, so
    ∠BCD + ∠ABC = 180°
    ∠BCD = 180° − 45° = 135°

There's often more than one way
of tackling these questions —
e.g. you could have found angle
BDC using the properties of
parallel lines, then used angles
in a triangle to find BCD.

EXAMPLE: The hexagon in the diagram is regular.
Find the size of the angle DGJ.

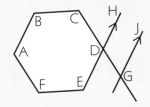

1) The hexagon is regular and ∠CDH is
    one of its exterior angles:

    $$\angle CDH = \frac{360°}{6} = 60°$$

2) Then using corresponding angles...

    ∠DGJ = ∠CDH = 60°

Missing: angle x. If found, please return to Amy...

Geometry problems often look a lot worse
than they are — don't panic, just write down
everything you can work out. Watch out for
hidden parallel lines and isosceles triangles
— they can help you work out angles.

Q1 Find the size of angle x.

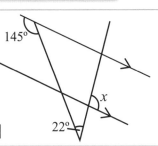

[3 marks]

Circle Geometry

After all that babble about lines and polygons, it's now time to get circular — how groovy...
Get ready for a 2-page extravaganza all about circle theorems.

8 ~~Simple~~ Rules to Learn

1) A TANGENT and a RADIUS meet at 90°.

A TANGENT is a line that just touches a single point on the circumference of a circle.
A tangent always makes an angle of exactly 90° with the radius it meets at this point.

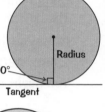

Radius

90°

Tangent

2) TWO RADII form an ISOSCELES TRIANGLE.

Radii is the plural of radius.

Unlike other isosceles triangles they don't have the little tick marks on the sides
to remind you that they are the same — the fact that they are both radii is
enough to make it an isosceles triangle.

3) The PERPENDICULAR BISECTOR of a CHORD passes through the CENTRE of the circle.

A CHORD is any line drawn across a circle. And no matter
where you draw a chord, the line that cuts it exactly in half
(at 90°), will go through the centre of the circle.

Perpendicular bisector

O

Chord

4) The angle at the CENTRE of a circle is TWICE the angle at the CIRCUMFERENCE.

The angle subtended at the centre of a circle is EXACTLY DOUBLE
the angle subtended at the circumference of the circle from the
same two points (two ends of the same chord).

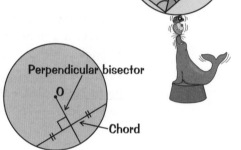

a

2a

'Angle subtended at'
is just a posh way of
saying 'angle made at'.

5) The ANGLE in a SEMICIRCLE is 90°.

A triangle drawn from the two ends of a diameter
will ALWAYS make an angle of 90° where it hits the
circumference of the circle, no matter where it hits.

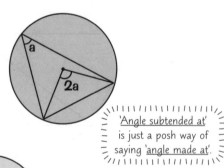

6) Angles in the SAME SEGMENT are EQUAL.

All triangles drawn from a chord will have the same angle
where they touch the circumference. Also, the two angles
on opposite sides of the chord add up to 180°.

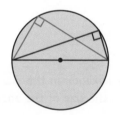

b

b

Chord

a

a

$a+b = 180°$

7) OPPOSITE ANGLES in a CYCLIC QUADRILATERAL add up to 180°.

A cyclic quadrilateral is a 4-sided shape with every corner touching
the circle. Both pairs of opposite angles add up to 180°.

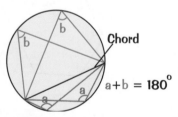

a

b

d

c

$a + c = 180°$
$b + d = 180°$

What? No Exam Practice Questions? I feel cheated.

Circle Geometry

Another circle theorem? But I've had enough. Can't I go home now?

The Final Rule to Learn

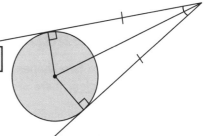

8) TANGENTS from the SAME POINT are the SAME LENGTH.

Two tangents drawn from an outside point are
<u>always equal in length</u>, creating <u>two congruent</u>
<u>right-angled triangles</u> as shown.

*Congruent means
exactly the same.*

Using the Circle Theorems

EXAMPLE: The diagram shows the triangle ABC, where lines BA and BC are
tangents to the circle. Show that line AC is NOT a diameter.

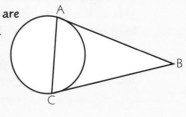

If AC was a diameter passing through the centre, O, then OA and
OC would be radii, and angle CAB = angle ACB = 90° by rule 1:

1) A TANGENT and a RADIUS meet at 90°.

However, this would mean that ABC isn't a triangle as you can't
have a triangle with two 90° angles, so AC cannot be a diameter.

*If angles CAB and ACB were
90°, lines AB and BC would be
parallel so would never meet.*

EXAMPLE: The lines AB and DE are tangents to the circle, centred at O,
at the points C and F respectively. The angle ACF is 79°.
Find the size of the shaded angle DFC.

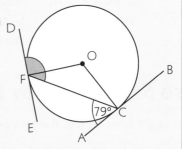

You'll probably have to use more than one rule to solve circle theorem
questions — here, AB is a <u>tangent</u> so use rule 1:

1) A TANGENT and a RADIUS meet at 90°.

So angle OCF = 90° − 79° = 11°.

Then find the other angle in the triangle by using rule 2:

2) TWO RADII form an ISOSCELES TRIANGLE.

Since OF and OC are <u>two radii</u>, the triangle is <u>isosceles</u> and **angle OFC = angle OCF = 11°**

Now just use rule 1 again on the on the <u>tangent</u> DE:

1) A TANGENT and a RADIUS meet at 90°.

Angle DFO = 90° and so **angle DFC = angle DFO + angle OFC = 90° + 11° = 101°**

All this talk of segments and tangerines is making me hungry...

Learn <u>all 8 rules</u> and practise using them — sometimes the best approach
is to try different rules until you find one that works.

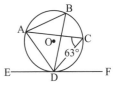

Q1   A, B, C and D are points on the circumference of the circle with centre O.
The line EF is a tangent to the circle, and touches the circle at D.
Angle ACD is 63°. Find the size of angle ABD.   [1 mark]

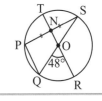

Q2   P, Q, R, S and T are points of the circumference of the circle with centre O.
The line QS is a diameter of the circle and the line RT is the
perpendicular bisector of the chord PS. The angle QOR is 48°.
Find the size of the angles PSQ and PQS.   [3 marks]

Similarity

Similar shapes are exactly the same shape, but can be different sizes (they can also be rotated or reflected).

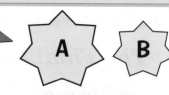

Similar Shapes Have the Same Angles

Generally, for two shapes to be similar, all the angles must match and the sides must be proportional. But for triangles, there are three special conditions — if any one of these is true, you know they're similar.

Two triangles are similar if:

1) **All the angles match up** i.e. the angles in one triangle are the same as the other.

2) **All three sides are proportional** i.e. if one side is twice as long as the corresponding side in the other triangle, all the sides are twice as long as the corresponding sides.

3) **Any two sides are proportional and the angle between them is the same.**

> Watch out — if one of the triangles has been rotated or flipped over, it might look as if they're not similar, but don't be fooled.

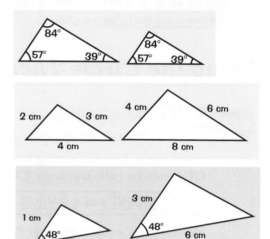

EXAMPLE: Show that triangles ABC and ADE are similar.

∠ BAC = ∠ EAD (vertically opposite angles)

∠ ABC = ∠ ADE (alternate angles)

∠ BCA = ∠ AED (alternate angles)

> See p.36 for more on angles around parallel lines.

The angles in triangle ABC are the same as the angles in triangle ADE, so the triangles are similar.

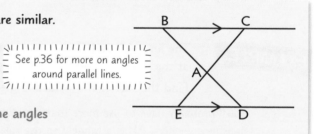

Use Similarity to Find Missing Lengths

You might have to use the properties of similar shapes to find missing distances, lengths etc.

You'll need to use scale factors to find the lengths of missing sides — use $\text{scale factor} = \dfrac{\text{new length}}{\text{old length}}$.

EXAMPLE: Suzanna is swimming in the sea. When she is at point B, she is 20 m from a rock that is 8 m tall at its highest point. There is a lighthouse 50 m away from Suzanna that is directly behind the rock. From her perspective, the top of the lighthouse is in line with the top of the rock. How tall is the lighthouse?

The triangles formed between Suzanna and the rock and Suzanna and the lighthouse are similar, so work out the scale factor: $\text{scale factor} = \dfrac{50}{20} = 2.5$

Now use the scale factor to work out the height of the lighthouse: $\text{height} = 8 \times 2.5 = 20$ m

Butter and margarine — similar products...

Be careful when working out the scale factor. If the length you're finding is bigger than the one you know, the scale factor should be greater than 1. If it's the other way round, the scale factor should be less than 1.

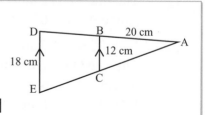

Q1 Find the length of DB. [2 marks]

Section Three — Geometric Skills

Arcs and Sectors

Before we crack on with the area of circles and their sectors, here's a recap of some easy <u>area formulas</u>:

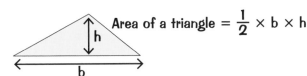

Area of a triangle $= \frac{1}{2} \times b \times h$

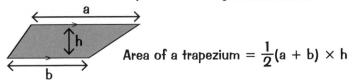

Area of a trapezium $= \frac{1}{2}(a + b) \times h$

Area *and* Circumference *of Circles*

You might already know these <u>important formulas</u>. If not, you'll need to learn them.

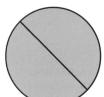

<u>Area of circle</u> $= \pi \times (\text{radius})^2$
Remember that the <u>radius</u> is <u>half</u> the <u>diameter</u>.

$$A = \pi r^2$$

<u>Circumference</u> $= \pi \times \text{diameter}$
$= 2 \times \pi \times \text{radius}$

$$C = \pi D = 2\pi r$$

For these formulas, use the π button on your <u>calculator</u>. For non-calculator questions, use $\pi \approx 3.14$ (unless the question tells you otherwise). If you're told to give an <u>exact</u> answer, leave your answer in <u>terms of π</u>.

Areas *of Sectors* and Lengths *of Arcs*

These ones are trickier — make sure you know the formulas, and what a <u>sector</u> and an <u>arc</u> are.

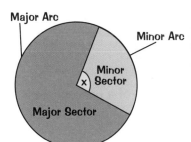

Major Arc

Minor Arc

Minor Sector

x

Major Sector

$$\underline{\text{Area of Sector}} = \frac{x}{360} \times \text{Area of Full Circle}$$

(Pretty obvious really, isn't it?)

$$\underline{\text{Length of Arc}} = \frac{x}{360} \times \text{Circumference of Full Circle}$$

(Obvious again, no?)

EXAMPLE: Two identical windscreen wipers are fixed at points O and P respectively, as shown below. They each move along the arc of a circle.

The windscreen wipers each have a length of 55 cm and the length of each arc is 92.6 cm.

Find: a) the size of the angle through which a wiper turns,
b) the total area of the windscreen cleared by the wipers, given that the area where the two wipers overlap is 550 cm².

a) You're given the <u>arc length</u> and the <u>radius</u> of the circle, so <u>rearrange</u> the formula to find the angle.

$$92.6 = \frac{x}{360} \times (2\pi \times 55)$$

$$x = \frac{92.6 \times 360}{2\pi \times 55}$$

$$= 96.465...°$$

$$= 96.5° \text{ (1 d.p.)}$$

b) The area covered by one wiper is the area of the <u>sector</u>:

$$A = \frac{96.465...}{360} \times (\pi \times 55^2)$$

$$= 2546.5 \text{ cm}^2$$

Always use the exact, unrounded values in your calculations.

So the area covered by <u>both</u> windscreen wipers is <u>double</u> this:

$$2A = 2 \times 2546.5 = 5093 \text{ cm}^2$$

But this has counted the overlap <u>twice</u>.
So subtract 550 (the area of the overlap):

Total area $= 5093 - 550 = 4543 \text{ cm}^2$

Pi r not square — pi are round. Pi are tasty...

Learn the sector and arc formulas and you're onto a winner — but remember that if you're asked for the <u>perimeter</u> of a sector, you need to include the straight edges as well the arc.

Q1 For the sector on the right, find to 2 decimal places:
  a) the area   [3 marks]   b) the arc length   [3 marks]

4 cm   112°

Volume

Two whole pages on <u>volumes</u> of <u>3D shapes</u> — aren't you lucky? I'm fairly certain that you already know that the volume of a <u>cuboid</u> is length × breadth × height (and of a <u>cube</u> is length³) — if not, you do now.

Volumes of Prisms

<u>A PRISM</u> is a solid (3D) object which is the same shape all the way through — i.e. it has a <u>CONSTANT AREA OF CROSS-SECTION</u>.

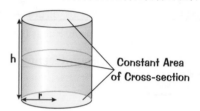

You've probably come across these shapes before. Watch out for them turning up in combination with other shapes.

$$\begin{array}{c} \text{VOLUME} \\ \text{OF PRISM} \end{array} = \begin{array}{c} \text{CROSS-SECTIONAL} \\ \text{AREA} \end{array} \times \text{LENGTH} \qquad \boxed{V = A \times L}$$

Triangular Prism

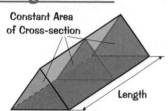

Constant Area of Cross-section

Length

Cylinder

Here, the cross-sectional area is a <u>circle</u>, so the formula for the volume of a <u>cylinder</u> is:

$$\boxed{V = \pi r^2 h}$$

h

Constant Area of Cross-section

r

Volumes of Spheres

$$\text{VOLUME OF SPHERE} = \frac{4}{3}\pi r^3$$

A <u>hemisphere</u> is half a sphere. So the volume of a hemisphere is just half the volume of a full sphere, $V = \frac{2}{3}\pi r^3$.

EXAMPLE:

A flagpole is made from a cylinder with a hemisphere on the top, as shown in the diagram.

The total height of the flagpole is 5 m and the diameter is 20 cm.

Find the volume of the flagpole in cm³, to 3 significant figures.

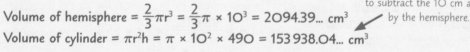

20 cm

5 m

1) First, put everything in terms of the <u>same units</u>. The question asks for cm³ so use centimetres.

Diameter = 20 cm, Height = 5 m = (5 × 100) cm = 500 cm

2) Then calculate the volume of each of the <u>individual shapes</u>.
The radius is 20 ÷ 2 = 10 cm:

The height of the cylinder is only 490 cm — don't forget to subtract the 10 cm added by the hemisphere.

Volume of hemisphere = $\frac{2}{3}\pi r^3 = \frac{2}{3}\pi \times 10^3 = 2094.39...$ cm³

Volume of cylinder = $\pi r^2 h = \pi \times 10^2 \times 490 = 153\,938.04...$ cm³

3) The <u>total volume</u> is the sum of these:

Volume of flagpole = 153 938.04... + 2094.39... = 156 032.43... = 156 000 cm³ (3 s.f.)

I bet you've had a ball with this page — you're really on a roll...

Volume questions often involve different bits of solids stuck together to create other shapes. You might be given a diagram in the exam to help — but if not, go ahead and draw your own.

Q1 The diagram to the right shows a Newton's cradle.

It consists of 5 swinging spheres, each with a radius of 6 mm, a cuboid base of dimensions 250 mm × 100 mm × 20 mm and six identical cylindrical posts, each of diameter 5 mm and length 200 mm.

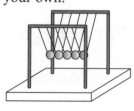

Find the volume of the entire Newton's cradle to 3 significant figures. You may assume the strings holding the spheres have no volume.

[5 marks]

Volume

Another page on volumes now. First up, it's volumes of cones, then it's on to cones with a bit <u>chopped off</u>.

Volumes of Pyramids and Cones

A pyramid is a shape that goes from a <u>flat base</u> up to a <u>point</u> at the top. Its base can be any shape at all. If the base is a circle then it's called a <u>cone</u> (rather than a circular pyramid).

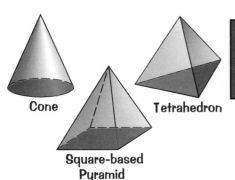

Cone   Tetrahedron

Square-based
Pyramid

> **VOLUME OF PYRAMID** $= \frac{1}{3} \times$ **BASE AREA** $\times$ **VERTICAL HEIGHT**
>
> **VOLUME OF CONE** $= \frac{1}{3} \times \pi r^2 \times h$

Make sure you use the <u>vertical</u> (<u>perpendicular</u>) <u>height</u> in these formulas — that's the distance from the <u>centre of the base</u> to the <u>point</u>.

Volumes of Frustums

A <u>frustum of a cone</u> is what's left when the top part of a cone is cut off parallel to its circular base.

> **VOLUME OF** **FRUSTUM** $=$ **VOLUME OF** **ORIGINAL CONE** $-$ **VOLUME OF** **REMOVED CONE**
>
> $= \frac{1}{3}\pi R^2 H - \frac{1}{3}\pi r^2 h$

> The bit that's chopped off is a mini cone that's <u>similar</u> to the original cone.

This bit is the frustum

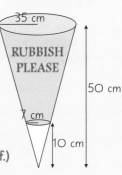

EXAMPLE: A waste paper basket is the shape of a frustum formed by removing a cone of height 10 cm, radius 7 cm from a cone of height 50 cm, radius 35 cm. Find the volume of the waste paper basket to 3 significant figures.

Volume of <u>original cone</u> $= \frac{1}{3}\pi R^2 H = \frac{1}{3} \times \pi \times 35^2 \times 50 = 64\,140.850...$ cm³

Volume of <u>removed cone</u> $= \frac{1}{3}\pi r^2 h = \frac{1}{3} \times \pi \times 7^2 \times 10 = 513.126...$ cm³

Volume of <u>frustum</u> $= 64\,140.850... - 513.126... = 63\,627.723... = 63\,600$ cm³ (3 s.f.)

35 cm
RUBBISH
PLEASE
50 cm
7 cm
10 cm

No, a cone isn't 'just as good' — all the other Pharaohs will laugh...

A common misconception is that a frustum is actually called a frustRum
(I thought this until about a year ago. It blew my mind.)

Q1   A cone and a sphere both have radius 9 cm. Their volumes are the same. Find the vertical height, h, of the cone.   [3 marks]

Q2   A square-based pyramid with base sides of length 60 cm and height 110 cm is filled with water. The water is then poured from the pyramid into a cone of the same height. The base of the cone has a diameter of 68 cm. Determine if the water overflows the cone.   [3 marks]

Using Similarity

You want to know how similarity from page 40 affects area and volume, you say? What a coincidence...

How Enlargement Affects Area and Volume

If a shape is enlarged by a <u>scale factor</u> (see page 40), its <u>area</u>, or <u>surface area</u> and <u>volume</u> (if it's a 3D shape), will change too. However, they <u>don't</u> change by the <u>same value</u> as the scale factor:

> For a <u>SCALE FACTOR</u> n:
>
> The <u>SIDES</u> are   n times bigger
> The <u>AREAS</u> are n^2 times bigger
> The <u>VOLUMES</u> are n^3 times bigger
>
> And:
>
> $n = \dfrac{\text{new length}}{\text{old length}}$ $n^2 = \dfrac{\text{new area}}{\text{old area}}$
>
> $n^3 = \dfrac{\text{new volume}}{\text{old volume}}$

So if the <u>scale factor</u> is <u>2</u>, the lengths are <u>twice as long</u>, the area is $2^2 = $ <u>4 times</u> as big, and the volume is $2^3 = $ <u>8 times</u> as big.

> **EXAMPLE:** Cylinder A has a height of 6 cm, and cylinder B has height of 18 cm. The volume of cylinder A is 2π cm³. Find the exact volume of cylinder B, given B is an enlargement of A.
>
> First, work out the <u>scale factor</u>, n: $n = \dfrac{\text{Height B}}{\text{Height A}} = \dfrac{18}{6} = 3$
>
> Use this in the volume formula: $n^3 = \dfrac{\text{Volume B}}{\text{Volume A}} \Rightarrow 3^3 = \dfrac{\text{Volume B}}{2\pi}$
>
> *Since you're asked for the exact volume, leave the answer in terms of π.*
>
> $\Rightarrow$ Volume of B $= 2\pi \times 27 = 54\pi$ cm³

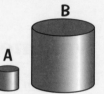

This shows that if the scale factor is <u>3</u>, lengths are <u>3 times as long</u> and the volume is <u>27 times as big</u> (and the area is <u>9 times as big</u>).

Proportionality is Linked to Similarity

If you know that the <u>price</u> of something is <u>proportional</u> to its area (or volume), you can work out the price of a <u>similar item</u> by multiplying or dividing by the <u>scale factor²</u> (or <u>scale factor³</u> for volume).

> **EXAMPLE:** The cost of a carpet is proportional to the area to be covered.
> Two mathematically similar rooms are to be carpeted.
> The length of the smaller room is 2 m and the length of the larger room is 7 m.
> If the cost to carpet the larger room is £918.75, calculate the cost to carpet the smaller room.
>
> First, work out the <u>scale factor</u> from the lengths: $n = \dfrac{7}{2} = 3.5$
>
> The price of the carpet is <u>proportional to area</u> so use <u>n²</u>.
> Since you're given the price of the larger room, you'll need to <u>divide</u> by the scale factor.
>
> Price for smaller room $= £918.75 \div 3.5^2$
> $= £918.75 \div 12.25$
> $= £75$

Twice as much learning, 4 times better results, 8 times more fun...

Make sure you don't get the scale factors mixed up — try them out on this Exam Practice Question.

Q1   There are 3 stacking dolls in a set. The dolls are mathematically similar and have heights of 5 cm, 10 cm and 15 cm. The volume of the middle doll is 216 cm³. Find the volume of smallest doll and the volume of the largest doll.   **[3 marks]**

Pythagoras' Theorem

Pythagoras' theorem sounds hard but it's actually <u>dead simple</u>.
It's also dead important, so make sure you really get your teeth into it.

Pythagoras' Theorem — $a^2 + b^2 = c^2$

1) <u>PYTHAGORAS' THEOREM</u> only works for <u>RIGHT-ANGLED TRIANGLES</u>.

2) Pythagoras uses <u>two sides</u> to find the <u>third side</u>.

3) The <u>BASIC FORMULA</u> for Pythagoras is $a^2 + b^2 = c^2$

4) Make sure you get the numbers in the <u>RIGHT PLACE</u>. c is the <u>longest side</u> (called the hypotenuse) and it's always <u>opposite</u> the right angle.

5) Always <u>CHECK</u> that your answer is <u>SENSIBLE</u>.

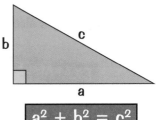

$$a^2 + b^2 = c^2$$

EXAMPLE:

ABC is a right-angled triangle.
AB = 6 m and AC = 3 m.
Find the exact length of BC.

1) Write down the <u>formula</u>. — $a^2 + b^2 = c^2$

2) Put in the <u>numbers</u>. — $BC^2 + 3^2 = 6^2$

3) <u>Rearrange</u> the equation. — $BC^2 = 6^2 - 3^2 = 36 - 9 = 27$

4) Take <u>square roots</u> to find BC. — $BC = \sqrt{27} = 3\sqrt{3}$ m

5) '<u>Exact length</u>' means you should give your answer as a <u>surd</u> — <u>simplified</u> if possible.

It's <u>not always c</u> you need to find — loads of people go wrong here.

Remember to check the answer's <u>sensible</u> — here it's about <u>5.2</u>, which is between <u>3 and 6</u>, so that seems about right...

Use Pythagoras to find the Distance Between Points

You need to know how to find the straight-line <u>distance</u> between <u>two points</u> on a <u>graph</u>.
If you get a question like this, follow these rules and it'll all become breathtakingly simple:

> 1) Draw a <u>sketch</u> to show the <u>right-angled triangle</u>.
> 2) Find the <u>lengths of the shorter sides</u> of the triangle by <u>subtracting</u> the <u>coordinates</u>.
> 3) <u>Use Pythagoras</u> to find the <u>length of the hypotenuse</u>. (That's your answer.)

EXAMPLE: Point P has coordinates (8, 3) and point Q has coordinates (−4, 8). Find the length of the line PQ.

①

② Length of <u>side a</u> = 8 − 3 = 5
Length of <u>side b</u> = 8 − −4 = 12

③ Use <u>Pythagoras</u> to find <u>side c</u>:
$c^2 = a^2 + b^2 = 5^2 + 12^2 = 25 + 144 = 169$
So: $c = \sqrt{169} = 13$

Remember, if it's not a right angle, it's a wrong angle...

Once you've learned all the Pythagoras facts on this page, try these Exam Practice Questions.

Q1 Find the length AC in the triangle to the right to 3 significant figures. [2 marks]

Q2 Point P has coordinates (10, 15) and point B has coordinates (6, 12).
Find the distance between P and Q. [3 marks]

Q3 A right-angled triangle has a hypotenuse of length $2\sqrt{10}$ cm. Give possible
lengths for the other two sides of the triangle, given that the lengths are integers. [3 marks]

Pythagoras' Theorem

That guy Pythagoras was such a gem, we're giving him another whole page...

If $a^2 + b^2 = c^2$ then the Triangle is Right-Angled

You know that if a triangle is <u>right-angled</u>, then its sides are related by Pythagoras' theorem.
The <u>converse</u> is also true — if $a^2 + b^2 = c^2$, then the triangle <u>must</u> be right-angled.

EXAMPLE: A triangle has sides of length 7 cm, 48.75 cm and 49.25 cm.
Is the triangle right-angled? Justify your answer.

<u>Find $a^2 + b^2$</u> — a and b should be the two shortest sides

$$7^2 + 48.75^2 = 49 + 2376.5625 = 2425.5625$$

<u>Find c^2</u> — c should be the longest side

$$49.25^2 = 2425.5625$$

<u>Compare the two values</u> — if they're equal, the triangle is right-angled.

$a^2 + b^2 = c^2$ so, by Pythagoras' theorem, the triangle is right-angled.

3D Pythagoras — $a^2 + b^2 + c^2 = d^2$

There's a similar theorem in <u>3D</u> too — you just <u>add</u> in the <u>extra length</u>.
For example, imagine you had the <u>cuboid</u> below...

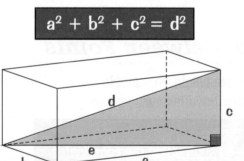

$$a^2 + b^2 + c^2 = d^2$$

In reality it's nothing you haven't seen before
— it's just <u>2D Pythagoras' theorem</u> being used <u>twice</u>:

1) <u>a, b and e</u> make a <u>right-angled triangle</u> so
$$e^2 = a^2 + b^2$$

2) Now look at the <u>right-angled triangle</u> formed by <u>e, c and d</u>:
$$d^2 = e^2 + c^2 = a^2 + b^2 + c^2$$

EXAMPLE: Find the exact length of the diagonal BH for the cube in the diagram.

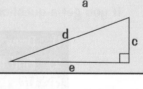

1) Write down the <u>formula</u>. $a^2 + b^2 + c^2 = d^2$

2) Put in the <u>numbers</u>. $4^2 + 4^2 + 4^2 = BH^2$

3) Take the <u>square root</u> to find BH. $\Rightarrow BH = \sqrt{48} = 4\sqrt{3}$ cm

3D Pythagoras can be used to find lengths in <u>other shapes</u> too — e.g. you might need it to work out the lengths in a square-based pyramid. See the next page for more on this.

Wow — just what can't right-angled triangles do...

Pythagoras questions appear in lots of different disguises — anything containing a right-angle is a likely suspect. They can pop up within circles — there's an example of this over on page 70.

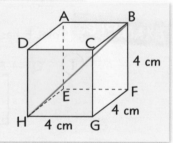

Q1   a)   Find the length AH in the cuboid shown to 3 s.f.   [3 marks]

     b)   The point P is the midpoint of FH. Determine whether the triangle BPC is right-angled. Justify your answer. [3 marks]

3D Coordinates

What could possible be more fun than 2D coordinates? 3D coordinates, that's what...

3D Space has a Z-Coordinate

All z-coordinates do is extend the normal x-y coordinates into a third direction, z, so that <u>all positions</u> then have <u>3 coordinates</u>: (x, y, z)

EXAMPLE: The diagram shows a cuboid.
Write down the coordinates of vertices B and F.

B has the same <u>x-</u> and <u>z-coordinates</u> as <u>A</u>, and the same <u>y-coordinate</u> as <u>C</u>.   B(7, 4, O)

F has the same <u>x-</u> and <u>y-coordinates</u> as <u>B</u> and the same <u>z-coordinate</u> as <u>H</u>.   F(7, 4, 2)

If it helps, you can write the lengths of the sides on the diagram.

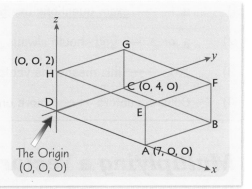

The Origin (O, O, O)

You Might Have to Use Some 3D Pythagoras

Glance back to pages 45-46 if you need a <u>refresher</u> of <u>Pythagoras' Theorem</u>. It'll come in handy here.

EXAMPLE: In the square-based pyramid shown, M is the midpoint of the base.
The vertex A lies directly above M.
E is the point (10, O, O), D is the point (18, O, O)
and AE has length $4\sqrt{6}$ units.
Find the length of AM and, hence, the coordinates of A.

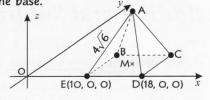

1) <u>Label N</u> as the midpoint of ED.
Then think of <u>EN, NM and AM</u> as three <u>sides</u> of a <u>cuboid</u>, and <u>AE</u> as the <u>longest diagonal</u> in the cuboid.

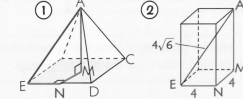

2) Sketch the <u>full cuboid</u>.
ED = 18 − 10 = 8
EN = NM = 8 ÷ 2 = 4 (since the <u>base is square</u> and M is the <u>midpoint</u>).

3) Write down the <u>3D Pythagoras formula</u>, <u>rewrite</u> it using <u>side labels</u> and put in the <u>numbers</u> and <u>solve for AM</u>.

$a^2 + b^2 + c^2 = d^2$
$EN^2 + NM^2 + AM^2 = AE^2$
$\Rightarrow 4^2 + 4^2 + AM^2 = (4\sqrt{6})^2$
$\Rightarrow AM = \sqrt{96-16-16} = \sqrt{64} = 8$ units

4) Use the <u>known coordinates</u> and lengths to find the <u>coordinates of A</u>.

$z = AM = 8$
$x = OE + EN = 10 + 4 = 14$
$y = NM = 4$, so A(14, 4, 8)

A 3D shape, drawn on 2D paper? What sorcery is this...

Getting your head around the coordinates of 3D shapes can be a bit tricky.
Don't panic, just take your time.

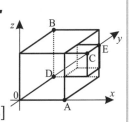

Q1   The diagram shows a cube attached to a larger cuboid. The point A has coordinates (3, 0, 0), the point B has coordinates (0, 4, 5) and the point C has coordinates (4, 0, 5). Write down the coordinates of D and E.   [2 marks]

Vectors

Vectors represent a movement of a certain <u>size</u> in a certain <u>direction</u>.
They might seem a bit weird at first, but there are really just a few facts to get to grips with...

The Vector Notations

There are several ways to <u>write</u> vectors...

1) **a** —— <u>exam questions</u> use <u>bold</u> like this

2) <u>a</u> or <u>a</u> — <u>you</u> should always <u>underline</u> them

3) $\overrightarrow{AB}$ —— this means the vector <u>from point A to point B</u>

4) Column vectors —— more on that on the <u>next page</u>

They're represented on a diagram by an <u>arrow</u>.

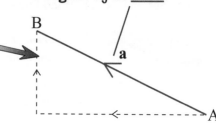

Multiplying a Vector by a Scalar

Multiplying a vector by a <u>positive</u> number <u>changes</u> the vector's <u>size</u> but <u>not its direction</u> — it <u>scales</u> the vector. If the number's <u>negative</u> then the <u>direction gets switched</u> and the <u>size</u> changes too (unless the scalar is –1).

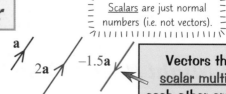

Scalars are just normal numbers (i.e. not vectors).

Vectors that are <u>scalar multiples</u> of each other are <u>parallel</u>.

Adding and Subtracting Vectors

You can describe movements between points by <u>adding</u> and <u>subtracting known vectors</u>.
Loads of vector <u>exam questions</u> are based around this.

"<u>a</u> + <u>b</u>" means 'go along <u>a</u> then <u>b</u>'.

"<u>c</u> – <u>d</u>" means 'go along <u>c</u> then backwards along <u>d</u>' (the <u>minus</u> sign means go the <u>opposite</u> way).

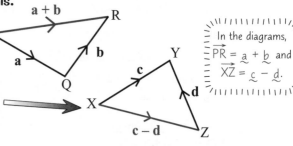

In the diagrams, $\overrightarrow{PR}$ = <u>a</u> + <u>b</u> and $\overrightarrow{XZ}$ = <u>c</u> – <u>d</u>.

EXAMPLE:

In the diagram below, M is the midpoint of BC.
Find vectors $\overrightarrow{AM}$, $\overrightarrow{OC}$ and $\overrightarrow{AC}$ in terms of a, b and m.

To obtain the <u>unknown vector</u> just '<u>get there</u>' by any route <u>made up of known vectors</u>.

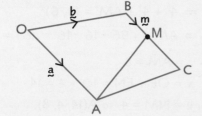

$\overrightarrow{AM}$ = –<u>a</u> + <u>b</u> + <u>m</u> —— A to M via O and B

$\overrightarrow{OC}$ = <u>b</u> + 2<u>m</u> —— O to C via B and M — M's half-way between B and C so $\overrightarrow{BC}$ = 2<u>m</u>

$\overrightarrow{AC}$ = –<u>a</u> + <u>b</u> + 2<u>m</u> —— A to C via O, B and M

From numpty to vector king — via R, E, V, I, S, I, O and N...

You need to get to grips with questions like the one above, so here's one to have a go at...

Q1 In triangle ABC, M is the midpoint of BC and N is the midpoint of AB. $\overrightarrow{AC}$ = **p** and $\overrightarrow{BM}$ = **q**. Find $\overrightarrow{AB}$ and $\overrightarrow{NA}$ in terms of **p** and **q**.

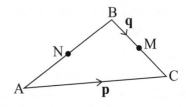

[2 marks]

Vectors

So far, you've seen vectors written as <u>directed line segments</u>. But they also come in another form...

Column Vectors are Made Up of Components

Vectors can also be represented by <u>components</u> — you describe how many
units to move <u>horizontally</u> and <u>vertically</u> and write it in a <u>column</u>.

For example: $\begin{pmatrix} 2 \\ -5 \end{pmatrix}$ — 2 units right, 5 units down $\qquad \begin{pmatrix} -7 \\ 4 \end{pmatrix}$ — 7 units left, 4 units up

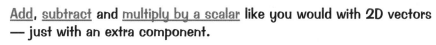

EXAMPLE: Find $\begin{pmatrix} 3 \\ -1 \end{pmatrix} + \begin{pmatrix} 5 \\ 3 \end{pmatrix}$ and $5\begin{pmatrix} 3 \\ -1 \end{pmatrix}$.

$$\begin{pmatrix} 3 \\ -1 \end{pmatrix} + \begin{pmatrix} 5 \\ 3 \end{pmatrix} = \begin{pmatrix} 8 \\ 2 \end{pmatrix} \qquad 5\begin{pmatrix} 3 \\ -1 \end{pmatrix} = \begin{pmatrix} 15 \\ -5 \end{pmatrix}$$

If you're given vectors on a <u>grid</u>, count the number of squares
<u>left/right</u> and <u>up/down</u> to find the components.

When <u>adding column vectors</u>, add the <u>top</u> to the <u>top</u> and
the <u>bottom</u> to the <u>bottom</u>. The same goes when <u>subtracting</u>.

To multiply a column vector by a <u>scalar</u>, just multiply <u>each component</u> by the scalar.
If the scalar's <u>negative</u>, it <u>changes the sign</u> of each component.

3D Vectors have a Third Component

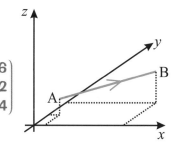

Vectors work pretty much <u>the same</u> in <u>three dimensions</u> —
see page 47 if you're not sure about 3D coordinates.
The only difference is that you put a <u>third number</u> in the column: $\vec{AB} = \begin{pmatrix} 6 \\ 2 \\ 4 \end{pmatrix}$

<u>Add</u>, <u>subtract</u> and <u>multiply by a scalar</u> like you would with 2D vectors
— just with an extra component.

Magnitude = |AB|

The <u>magnitude</u> of a vector is just its <u>length</u>. You find it using <u>Pythagoras</u> (see p.45).

E.g. for the vector $\vec{AB} = \begin{pmatrix} -7 \\ 4 \end{pmatrix}$: $\quad |\vec{AB}| = \left|\begin{pmatrix} -7 \\ 4 \end{pmatrix}\right| = \sqrt{(-7)^2 + 4^2} = \sqrt{65} = 8.1$ (1 d.p.)

It's the same for 3D vectors: $\left\|\begin{pmatrix} 6 \\ 2 \\ 4 \end{pmatrix}\right\| = \sqrt{6^2 + 2^2 + 4^2} = \sqrt{56} = 7.5$ (1 d.p.)

This is just 3D Pythagoras — see page 46.

EXAMPLE: Given the vectors $\underset{\sim}{a} = \begin{pmatrix} 3 \\ 9 \\ -1 \end{pmatrix}$ and $\underset{\sim}{b} = \begin{pmatrix} 10 \\ 0 \\ 1 \end{pmatrix}$, find the magnitude of the resultant vector $\underset{\sim}{a} + \underset{\sim}{b}$.

Give your answer as a surd in its simplest form.

A <u>resultant</u> vector is just a <u>sum</u> of vectors.

1) First find **a** + **b**:
$$\begin{pmatrix} 3 \\ 9 \\ -1 \end{pmatrix} + \begin{pmatrix} 10 \\ 0 \\ 1 \end{pmatrix} = \begin{pmatrix} 13 \\ 9 \\ 0 \end{pmatrix}$$

2) Then find the magnitude:
$$|\underset{\sim}{a} + \underset{\sim}{b}| = \left\|\begin{pmatrix} 13 \\ 9 \\ 0 \end{pmatrix}\right\| = \sqrt{13^2 + 9^2 + 0^2} = \sqrt{250} = \sqrt{25 \times 10} = 5\sqrt{10}$$

Never before has there been a topic of this magnitude...

You see, components aren't all that bad. Just deal with each of top and bottom (and middle if it's 3D)
one at a time. And the magnitude is nothing new — Pythagoras rearing his pretty little head again...

Q1 a) Write the vectors **u** and **v** shown
in the diagram in component form. [2 marks]

b) Find $\left|\frac{1}{2}\mathbf{u} - 2\mathbf{v}\right|$ to 2 decimal places. [3 marks]

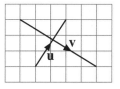

Revision Questions for Section Three

There are lots of opportunities to show off your artistic skills here (as long as you use them to answer the questions).

- Try these questions and <u>tick off each one</u> when you <u>get it right</u>.
- When you've done <u>all the questions</u> for a topic and are <u>completely happy</u> with it, tick off the topic.

Geometry (p35-37) ☐

1) What do the angles in a triangle add up to? What about the angles in a quadrilateral? ☑

2) What is the size of any angle in an equilateral triangle? ☑

3) What are the key features of a rhombus? What about a kite? ☑

4) Name the four different types of angles you find around parallel lines. ☑

5) Find the missing angles in the diagrams below.

a)  b) 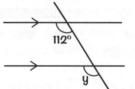 c) 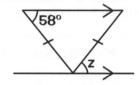 ☑

6) Find the exterior angle of a regular octagon. ☑

7) What do the interior angles of a nonagon (9-sided polygon) add up to? ☑

Circle Geometry (p38-39) ☐

8) Write down the eight rules of circle geometry. ☑

9) Find the missing angle in each of the diagrams below.

a) 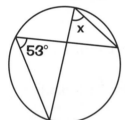 b) 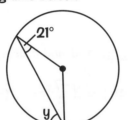 c) 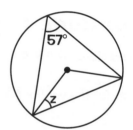 ☑

10) Exactly one of the quadrilaterals A and B below is cyclic.
Find the missing angle in the cyclic quadrilateral and explain why the other cannot be cyclic. ☑

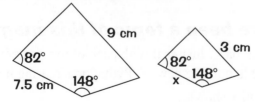

Similarity, Arcs and Sectors (p40-p41) ☐

11) State the three conditions you can use to prove that two triangles are similar. ☑

12) The shapes below are similar. What is the length of side x?

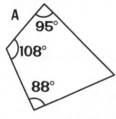

13) A circle has diameter 16 cm. Find its exact circumference and area. ☑

14) Find the area of the sector with radius 10 cm and angle 45° to 2 d.p. ☑

15) The perimeter of a sector is 10 cm. If the arc has length 4 cm, find the angle of the sector. ☑

Revision Questions for Section Three

Volume and Using Similarity (p42-44)

16) The cross-section of a prism is a regular hexagon with side length 6 cm.
The length of the prism is 11 cm. Find its volume to 3 s.f.

17) Find the exact volumes of the shapes below.

a)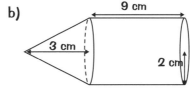

b)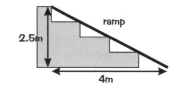

18) A shape with area 5 cm² is enlarged by a scale factor of 4. What is the area of the enlarged shape?

Pythagoras' Theorem (p45-46)

19) What is the formula for Pythagoras' theorem? What do you use it for?

20) A museum has a flight of stairs up to its front door (see diagram).
A ramp is to be put over the top of the steps for wheelchair users.
Calculate the length that the ramp would need to be to 3 s.f.

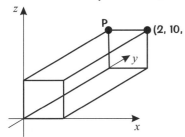

21) Point P has coordinates (–3, –2) and point Q has coordinates (2, 4).
Calculate the length of the line PQ to 1 d.p.

22) What is the formula for finding the length of the longest diagonal in a cuboid?

23) Find the length of the longest diagonal in the cuboid measuring 5 m × 6 m × 9 m.

3D Coordinates and Vectors (p47-49)

24) In each of the 3D shapes below, find the coordinates of the point P.

a)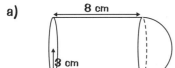

b)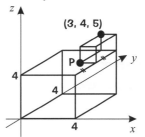

25) The cone on the right has its vertex on the origin and a radius of 2.
Given that the volume of the cone is 4π,
what are the coordinates of the centre of the cone's base?

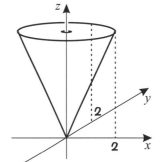

26) The triangle UVW is shown below. X is the midpoint of UW.
$\overrightarrow{XU} = \underset{\sim}{u}$, $\overrightarrow{XV} = \underset{\sim}{v}$. Find: a) $\overrightarrow{UV}$, b) $\overrightarrow{WV}$.

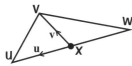

27) What is the effect of multiplying a vector by a scalar?

28) $\underset{\sim}{a}$ and $\underset{\sim}{b}$ are column vectors, where $\underset{\sim}{a} = \begin{pmatrix} 4 \\ -2 \end{pmatrix}$ and $\underset{\sim}{b} = \begin{pmatrix} 7 \\ 6 \end{pmatrix}$.

a) Find: (i) $\underset{\sim}{a} - \underset{\sim}{b}$ (ii) $5\underset{\sim}{a}$
(iii) $3\underset{\sim}{a} + \underset{\sim}{b}$ (iv) $-4\underset{\sim}{a} - 2\underset{\sim}{b}$

b) Find the exact magnitude of: (i) $\underset{\sim}{a}$, (ii) $\underset{\sim}{b}$, (iii) $\underset{\sim}{a} - \underset{\sim}{b}$.
You should simplify your answers as far as possible.

29) If $\underset{\sim}{p} = \begin{pmatrix} 4 \\ 2 \\ -2 \end{pmatrix}$, find the exact values of $\frac{1}{2}|\underset{\sim}{p}|$ and $|\frac{1}{2}\underset{\sim}{p}|$.

Trigonometric Graphs

Before you leave this page, you should be able to close your eyes and picture these three graphs in your head, <u>properly labelled</u> and everything. If you can't, you need to learn them more. I'm not kidding.

Sine 'Waves' and Cos 'Buckets'

1) The underlying shape of the sin and cos graphs is <u>identical</u> — they both bounce between <u>y-limits of exactly +1 and –1</u>.

2) The only difference is that the <u>sin graph</u> is <u>shifted right by 90°</u> compared to the cos graph.

Sin and cos have a <u>max</u> of 1 and a <u>min</u> of –1.

3) <u>For 0°-360°</u>, the shapes you get are a <u>Sine 'Wave'</u> (one peak, one trough) and a <u>Cos 'Bucket'</u> (starts at the top, dips, and finishes at the top).

4) Sin and cos <u>repeat</u> every <u>360°</u>. The distance from a point to the equivalent point on the next repetition is called the <u>period</u> (so here it's 360°).

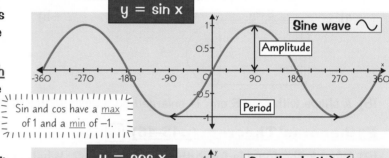

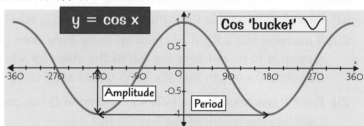

5) The key to drawing the extended graphs is to first draw the 0°-360° cycle of either the <u>Sine 'WAVE'</u> or the <u>Cos 'BUCKET'</u> and then <u>repeat it</u> forever in <u>both directions</u> as shown above.

6) The <u>amplitude</u> is <u>half the distance</u> from the <u>peak</u> to the <u>trough</u>. As the sin and cos graphs have a <u>maximum value</u> of <u>1</u> and a <u>minimum value</u> of <u>–1</u>, this is $\frac{1}{2}(1 - (-1)) = 1$.

Tan x can be Any Value at all

tan x is <u>different</u> from sin x or cos x — it goes between $-\infty$ and $+\infty$ (so its <u>amplitude</u> is <u>undefined</u>).

Tan x repeats every 180°

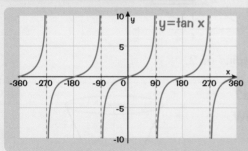

tan x goes from $-\infty$ to $+\infty$ every 180°, so it has a <u>period</u> of <u>180°</u>.

This means it <u>repeats</u> every 180° and takes <u>every possible</u> value in each 180° interval.

tan x is <u>undefined</u> at ±90°, ±270°,...

As you approach one of these undefined points from the left, tan x just shoots up to <u>infinity</u>.

As you approach from the right, it drops to <u>minus infinity</u>.

The graph never ever touches these lines. But it does get infinitely close, if you see what I mean...

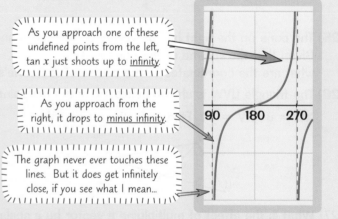

The easiest way to <u>sketch</u> any of these graphs is to plot the <u>important points</u> which happen every 90° (e.g. –180°, –90°, 0°, 90°, 180°, 270°, 360°, 450°, 540°...) and then just join the dots up.

The sine wave and the cos bucket — a great day out at the beach...

You could be asked to sketch any of these graphs. The trick is to learn the key points and shape of each graph. When you're ready, cover up the page and try out this here lil' question...

Q1   a)   Sketch the graph of $y = \cos x$ for values of x between –360° and 360°.   [2 marks]

         b)   Sketch the graph of $y = \sin x$ for values of x between 0° and 720°.   [2 marks]

Trigonometric Graphs

The next two pages cover all the types of transformations of trig graphs you'll need to know for your exam. We'll be using function notation (see page 21) for the trig functions — f(x) = sin x or f(x) = cos x.

If y = f(x) + c, the Graph Shifts in the y-Direction by c

1) This is where the whole graph is translated vertically (in the y-direction), and is achieved by adding a number onto the end of the equation, e.g. y = cos x + c.

2) The graph will move by c units — it moves up if c > 0 and down if c < 0.

> f(x) + c transforms
> (x, y) to (x, y + c)

EXAMPLE: The graphs of y = cos x + a and y = sin x + b are shown below. Determine the values of a and b.

Remember that cos is a bucket and sine is a wave so the top graph is cos and the bottom graph is sin.

The peak of each graph is usually at y = 1.

Since the peak of the cos graph is now at 3, it has been translated up 3 − 1 = 2 units.

So y = cos x + 2, i.e. a = 2.

The peak of the sin graph is now at y = 0, so it has been translated down by 1 − 0 = 1 unit.

So y = sin x − 1, i.e. b = −1.

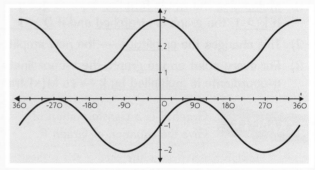

Phase Angles are Shifts in the x-Direction — y = f(x − c)

1) This is where the whole graph is translated left or right (in the x-direction) — it happens when you replace 'x' in the function with 'x − c'.

2) These can be confusing because they go the 'wrong way'. If you want to go from y = f(x) to y = f(x − c) you must move the whole graph a distance c in the positive x-direction → (i.e. right). Similarly, for y = f(x + c), the graph moves c units in the negative x-direction ← (i.e. left).

3) The value c is known as a phase angle.

> f(x − c) transforms
> (x, y) to (x + c, y)

EXAMPLE: The graph of y = sin x is shown below, for −360° ≤ x ≤ 360°.

a) Sketch the graph of sin (x − 60)° and write down the value of the phase angle.
y = sin (x − 60)° is y = sin x translated 60 units in the positive x-direction. The phase angle is just the value of the translation: **60°**

b) Give the coordinates of the points where y = sin (x − 60) crosses the x-axis for −360° ≤ x ≤ 360°.

Add 60° to the coordinates of the points where y = sin x crosses the axis: (−300, 0), (−120, 0), (60, 0), (240, 0)

More sliding and flipping than a martial arts film...

Make sure you don't get translations on the x- and y-axes mixed up. Now, practice question time...

Q1 On separate axes, sketch the graphs of the following functions for 0° ≤ x ≤ 360°:

a) 5 + cos x [2 marks] b) sin (x + 120)° [2 marks] c) 2 + sin (x − 180)° [3 marks]

Q2 Let A be the point with x-coordinate 90° on the graph of y = sin x. If the graph is translated by a phase angle of 200°, what are the x- and y-coordinates of the new position of A? [2 marks]

Trigonometric Graphs

The transformations on the last page <u>moved</u> the graphs of sin and cos around but left their <u>shapes</u> alone. Prepare to meet some transformations that have no qualms about <u>distorting</u> your favourite curves...

Reflections: $y = -f(x)$ and $y = f(-x)$

1) $y = -f(x)$ is the <u>reflection</u> in the <u>x-axis</u> of $y = f(x)$. So $y = \sin x$ would become $y = -\sin x$.

2) $y = f(-x)$ is the <u>reflection</u> in the <u>y-axis</u> of $y = f(x)$. So $y = \sin x$ would become $y = \sin(-x)$.

If $y = kf(x)$ then the Amplitude Changes

1) <u>Multiplying</u> the <u>whole function</u> by k to get $y = kf(x)$ <u>stretches</u> the graph <u>parallel to the y-axis</u>. If <u>k > 1</u>, the graph is <u>stretched</u> and if <u>0 < k < 1</u>, the graph is <u>squashed</u>.

   If k is <u>negative</u>, the graph is also reflected in the x-axis.

2) This changes the <u>amplitude</u> — the new amplitude is <u>k</u>.

3) For every point on the graph, the x-coordinate <u>stays the same</u>, and the y-coordinate is <u>multiplied by k</u> — so kf(x) transforms the point (x, y) to (x, ky).

 **EXAMPLE:** Graph R is a transformation of $y = \sin x$. Give the equation of Graph R.

Graph R is $y = \sin x$ <u>stretched in the vertical direction</u> — so it will be of the form $y = k \sin x$.
The peak is at $y = 3$ and the trough is at $y = -3$:
Amplitude = $(3 - (-3)) \div 2 = 6 \div 2 = 3$.
So the equation of Graph R is $y = 3 \sin x$.

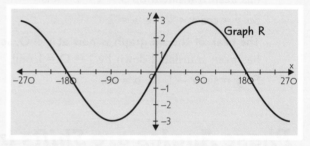

A Multiple Angle Changes the Period — $y = f(kx)$

1) A <u>multiple angle</u> is when the angle in the function (i.e. x) is <u>multiplied</u> by a number. So $y = \sin x$ becomes <u>$y = \sin kx$</u> (and the same for cos).

2) A multiple angle <u>stretches</u> the graph <u>parallel to the x-axis</u> by a scale factor of $\frac{1}{k}$. If <u>k > 1</u>, the graph is <u>squashed</u>. If <u>0 < k < 1</u>, the graph is <u>stretched</u>.

   If k is <u>negative</u>, the graph is also reflected in the y-axis.

3) This changes the <u>period</u> — the new period is <u>360 ÷ k</u>. In $0° \le x \le 360°$, there will be <u>k repetitions</u> of the sine <u>wave</u> or cos <u>bucket</u>.

4) The y-coordinate of each point <u>stays the same</u> and the x-coordinate is <u>multiplied by</u> $\frac{1}{k}$ — so f(kx) transforms the point (x, y) to ($\frac{x}{k}$, y).

 **EXAMPLE:** The graph of $y = \sin x$ is shown to the right. Sketch the graph $y = \sin 4x$ for $0° \le x \le 360°$.

sin 4x has a <u>multiple angle</u> so the <u>period</u> will change.
The new period is $360 \div 4 = 90°$ — the graph <u>repeats every 90°</u>.
This also means that the sin wave will <u>repeat 4 times</u> in the interval $0° \le x \le 360°$.

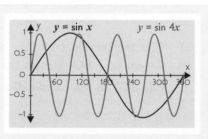

And stretch...   ... and breathe...   ...and relax...

Now you know about all these transformations, try them out on these Exam Practice Questions.

Q1   Sketch the graphs of $y = \cos 2x$ and $y = 2 \cos x$, $0° \le x \le 360°$, on the same set of axes.   [4 marks]

Q2   The graph of $y = p \sin qx$ (where p and q are positive integers) achieves its maximum value of $y = 5$ exactly 6 times in the interval $0° \le x \le 360°$. State the values of p and q.   [2 marks]

Trigonometry — Sin, Cos, Tan

You've probably seen this stuff before. You may already be an <u>expert</u> in Sin, Cos and Tan and proudly wear your <u>SOH CAH TOA</u> t-shirt, but it's worth going over it again — it'll <u>set you up</u> right for the rest of the section.

The 3 Trigonometry Formulas

There are three basic <u>trig formulas</u> — each one links <u>two sides and an angle</u> of a <u>right-angled triangle</u>.

$$\text{Sin } x = \frac{\text{Opposite}}{\text{Hypotenuse}}$$

$$\text{Cos } x = \frac{\text{Adjacent}}{\text{Hypotenuse}}$$

$$\text{Tan } x = \frac{\text{Opposite}}{\text{Adjacent}}$$

Use SOH CAH TOA to help you remember which trig functions go with which sides.

- The <u>Hypotenuse</u> is the <u>LONGEST SIDE</u>.

- The <u>Opposite</u> is the side <u>OPPOSITE</u> the angle <u>being used</u> (x).

- The <u>Adjacent</u> is the (other) side <u>NEXT TO</u> the angle <u>being used</u>.

Opposite (O) Hypotenuse (H) Adjacent (A) x

1) Whenever you come across a trig question, work out which <u>two sides</u> of the triangle are involved in that question — then <u>pick the formula</u> that involves those sides.

2) To <u>find the angle</u> — use the <u>inverse</u>, i.e. press **SHIFT** or **2ndF**, followed by <u>sin</u>, <u>cos</u> or <u>tan</u> (and make sure your calculator is in DEG mode) — your calculator will display <u>sin⁻¹</u>, <u>cos⁻¹</u> or <u>tan⁻¹</u>.

3) Remember, you can <u>only</u> use these formulas on <u>right-angled triangles</u> — you may have to <u>add lines</u> to the diagram to create one.

 **EXAMPLE:**

Find the angle x in this triangle to 1 d.p.

36 m   36 m x 40 m

It's an <u>isosceles</u> triangle so <u>split</u> it <u>down the middle</u> to get a <u>right-angled triangle</u>.

1) <u>Label</u> the three sides <u>O, A and H</u> (Opposite, Adjacent and Hypotenuse).

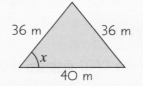

H   36 m   O x A   20 m

2) Write down <u>from memory</u> '<u>SOH CAH TOA</u>'.

SOH (CAH) TOA

3) Decide which <u>two sides</u> are <u>involved</u>: O,H A,H or O,A and select <u>SOH</u>, <u>CAH</u> or <u>TOA</u> accordingly — <u>A</u> and <u>H</u> are involved here.

4) Write down the <u>formula</u> you need. $C = \dfrac{A}{H}$

5) <u>Translate into numbers</u> and work it out.

$$\cos x = \frac{20}{36}$$

$$\Rightarrow x = \cos^{-1}\left(\frac{20}{36}\right) = 56.2510114...°$$
$$= 56.3° \text{ (1 d.p.)}$$

If you find it useful, you can turn SOH, CAH or TOA into a <u>formula triangle</u>:

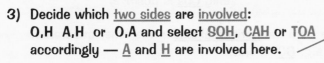

SOH — O / S×H   **CAH** — A / C×H   **TOA** — O / T×A

<u>Cover up</u> the thing you want to find and <u>write down</u> whatever is left showing.

SOH CAH TOA — the not-so-secret formula for success...

You need to know this stuff off by heart — so go over this page a few times until you've got those formulas firmly lodged and all ready to reel off in the exam. All set? Time for a question...

Q1 A ladder is leaning against a vertical wall. It is at an angle of 74° to the horizontal ground. The base of the ladder is on the ground 0.9 m away from the wall. How long is the ladder? Give your answer to 3 s.f. [2 marks]

Related Angles

If you use your <u>calculator</u> to solve a <u>trig equation</u>, it'll give you a value for x. But you can see from the graphs on page 52 that each trig function takes the same y-value <u>twice</u> in each 360° interval — peruse below to find out how to find the <u>other values</u>...

You Can Use the Graph...

1) Draw the <u>graph</u> of y = f(x) for the range you're interested in...
2) Get the first solution from your <u>calculator</u> and mark this on the graph.
3) Use the <u>symmetry of the graph</u> to work out what the other solutions are.

Say you had a y-value of $\frac{1}{2}$ (i.e. sin x = $\frac{1}{2}$, cos x = $\frac{1}{2}$ or tan x = $\frac{1}{2}$). Your <u>calculator</u> would give a value of x = <u>30</u>° for sin, x = <u>60</u>° for cos and x = <u>26.5...</u>° for tan. Use the graph to find the other value.

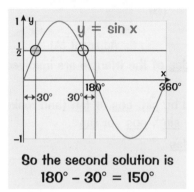

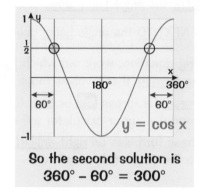

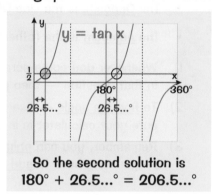

So the second solution is
180° – 30° = 150°

So the second solution is
360° – 60° = 300°

So the second solution is
180° + 26.5...° = 206.5...°

...or the CAST Diagram

<u>CAST</u> stands for <u>COS</u>, <u>ALL</u>, <u>SIN</u>, <u>TAN</u> — the CAST <u>diagram</u> shows you where these functions are <u>positive</u>:

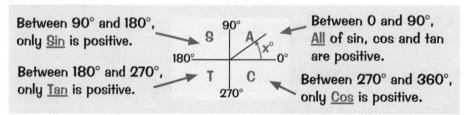

Between 90° and 180°,
only <u>Sin</u> is positive.

Between 180° and 270°,
only <u>Tan</u> is positive.

Between 0 and 90°,
<u>All</u> of sin, cos and tan
are positive.

Between 270° and 360°,
only <u>Cos</u> is positive.

To find the other angles, make the <u>same angle</u> from the <u>horizontal axis</u> in the other quadrants.
So, if your calculator gives you an x-value of e.g. <u>60</u>° then...

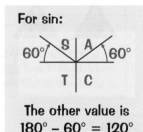

For sin:

The other value is
180° – 60° = 120°

For cos:

The other value is
360° – 60° = 120°

For tan:

The other value is
180° + 60° = 240°

When the angle from your calculator is <u>negative</u>, use the <u>quadrants</u> you <u>wouldn't</u> normally use. E.g. for sin, use the C and T quadrants.

You'll use all this in practice on the <u>next page</u> when you start solving some pesky <u>trig equations</u>...

Related angles are sinful (and cosful and tanful)...

Two methods here — try and understand them both if you can but make sure you have a least one of them fixed in your brain. Have a go at these Exam Practice Questions to see how things are going.

Q1 Find the values of x between 0° ≤ x ≤ 360° that satisfy tan x = 0.3. [2 marks]

Q2 Solve cos x = $-\frac{1}{4}$ in the range 0° ≤ x ≤ 360°. [2 marks]

Q3 Solve sin x = –0.5 for 0° ≤ x ≤ 360°. [2 marks]

Solving Trig Equations

Now that you know all about <u>related angles</u> (psst... read the previous page if you haven't already), it's about time you got your hands dirty and put all that new-gotten knowledge to use — off you go...

Use a Graph or CAST Diagram to find All the Solutions

 EXAMPLE: Solve $\tan x = -\dfrac{3}{2}$ for $0° \le x \le 360°$.

1) Use your <u>calculator</u>: $x = \tan^{-1}\left(-\dfrac{3}{2}\right)$

$x = -56.3099...°$ ⟵ *This solution isn't in the interval you're looking at.*

2) <u>Sketch</u> the graph of $y = \tan x$.
Make it <u>larger</u> than the <u>range</u> you want, so you can include the <u>angle</u> from your calculator.

3) Use the <u>period</u> of tan (<u>180°</u>) to work out the other <u>solutions</u>:

$x = -56.3099...° + 180° = 123.6901...° = 123.7°$ (1 d.p.)
$x = 123.6901... + 180° = 303.6901...° = 303.7°$ (1 d.p.)

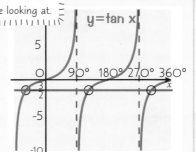

y=tan x

EXAMPLE: The graphs of $y = 5\cos x + 3$ and $y = 7$ in the range $0 \le x \le 360°$ are shown below. Find the x-coordinates of the points where they intersect in this range.

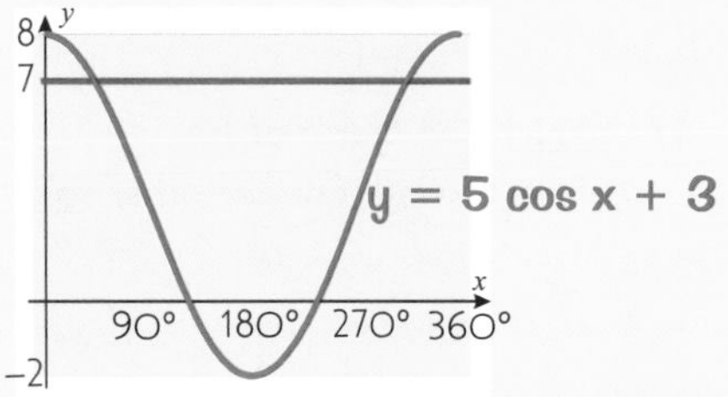

1) To find where two graphs intersect, set them <u>equal</u> to each other: $5\cos x + 3 = 7$

2) <u>Solve</u> the equation:

$5\cos x + 3 = 7$
$5\cos x = 4$
$\cos x = \dfrac{4}{5}$

The equation has to be in the form $\underline{\cos x = n}$ before you can solve it.

$x = \cos^{-1}\left(\dfrac{4}{5}\right)$

$= 36.86989...° = 36.9°$ (1 d.p.)

y = 5 cos x + 3

3) Use the <u>symmetry</u> of the <u>graph</u> to find the other solution: $x = 360° - 36.86989...°$
$= 323.1301...° = 323.1°$ (1 d.p.)

EXAMPLE: A housing estate is in the shape of a circle. A noisy power plant is adjacent to the estate. The noise level at different points on the estate can be modelled by $n = 10\sin p° + 60$, where n dB (decibels) is the noise level and $0 \le p \le 360$ is the clockwise angle a point makes with the vertical as shown in the diagram.

a) The point X makes the angle $p = 300°$. Find the noise level at X.
b) What is the greatest noise level on the estate?
c) Find the values of p for which the noise level is 65 dB.

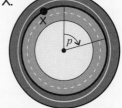

POWER PLANT

a) $n_x = 10\sin(300) + 60$
$= 51.3$ dB (1 d.p.)

b) The <u>highest</u> value sin can take is <u>1</u>:
$n_{max} = 10 \times 1 + 60$
$= 70$ dB

c) Let $n = 65$ and <u>solve</u> the equation:

$65 = 10\sin p + 60$
$5 = 10\sin p$
$\dfrac{1}{2} = \sin p$

$p = \sin^{-1}\left(\dfrac{1}{2}\right) = 30$

Using <u>CAST</u>: $p = 180 - 30 = 150$

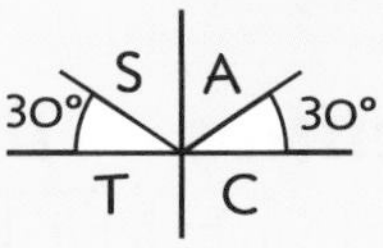

```
    S | A
30°   |   30°
    T | C
```

And I feel that love is dead, I'm loving angles instead...

Sketching a graph is a really useful way of seeing where the solutions are and how to find them.
Always check whether the answer given by your calculator is actually in the interval you want.

Q1   Solve $20\sin x + 3 = 10$ in the interval $0° \le x \le 360°$.   [3 marks]

Trig Identities

Now for something really exciting — trig identities. Mmm, well, maybe exciting was the wrong word.

Tan Can be Written in Terms of Sin and Cos

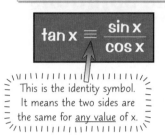

$$\tan x \equiv \frac{\sin x}{\cos x}$$

This is the identity symbol. It means the two sides are the same for any value of x.

This is a handy thing to know. The most likely places to use it are:

1) When you have a sin and cos and you can divide sin by cos, e.g. $5 \sin x = \cos x$

2) When you see a tan, together with a sin or a cos, e.g. $3 \cos x \tan x$.

EXAMPLE: Simplify $\frac{5 \sin x}{\tan x}$.

There's a sin and a tan so try using the identity.

$$\frac{5 \sin x}{\tan x} = \frac{5 \sin x}{\left(\frac{\sin x}{\cos x}\right)} = \frac{5 \sin x \cos x}{\sin x} = 5 \cos x$$

EXAMPLE: Solve $5 \sin x = \cos x$ for $0° \leq x \leq 360°$.

1) It's got sin and cos in it — so divide through by cos x. $\quad \frac{5 \sin x}{\cos x} = 1$

2) Now you can substitute in $\tan x = \frac{\sin x}{\cos x}$. $\quad 5 \tan x = 1$

3) Use your calculator to find the first solution. $\quad \tan x = \frac{1}{5}$

$$x = \tan^{-1}\left(\frac{1}{5}\right)$$
$$= 11.3099...°$$

4) Sketch the graph of $y = \tan x$, then use it to work out the other solutions.

$$x = 180° + 11.3099...°$$
$$= 191.3099...°$$

So $x = 11.3°, 191.3°$ (to 1 d.p.)

(graph of $y = \tan x$ shown with points at 0.2)

If You See Sin² or Cos², Think of This Identity...

$$\sin^2 x + \cos^2 x \equiv 1$$

...which can be rearranged to give...

$$\sin^2 x \equiv 1 - \cos^2 x$$
$$\cos^2 x \equiv 1 - \sin^2 x$$

Be careful — $\sin^2 x$ means $(\sin x)^2$, not $\sin(x^2)$.

EXAMPLE: Show that $\frac{\cos^2 x}{1 + \sin x} \equiv 1 - \sin x$

Prove things like this by playing about with one side of the equation until you get the other side.

The only thing I can think of doing here is replacing $\cos^2 x$ with $1 - \sin^2 x$. (Which is good because it works.)

The top line is a difference of two squares (p.15).

Left-hand side: $\frac{\cos^2 x}{1 + \sin x}$

$$\equiv \frac{1 - \sin^2 x}{1 + \sin x}$$

$$\equiv \frac{(1 + \sin x)(1 - \sin x)}{1 + \sin x}$$

$$\equiv 1 - \sin x, \text{ the right-hand side}$$

Trig identities — the path to a brighter future...

Those identities can be a bit daunting, but it's always worth having a few tricks in mind — look for things that factorise, or fractions that can be cancelled down, or ways to use those trig identities.

Q1 Solve $7 \tan x \cos x = 5$ in the interval $0° \leq x \leq 360°$. [3 marks]

Q2 Simplify $\cos^2 x \tan^2 x + \cos^2 x$ as far as possible. [2 marks]

Q3 Show that $\cos x + 1 \equiv \frac{\sin^2 x}{1 - \cos x}$. [3 marks] Q4 Simplify $\frac{3 \sin^2 x \tan x}{\cos^2 x}$. [2 marks]

The Sine and Cosine Rules

Normal trigonometry using **SOH CAH TOA** etc. can only be applied to <u>right-angled</u> triangles. Which leaves us with the question of what to do with other-angled triangles. Step forward the <u>Sine and Cosine Rules</u>...

Labelling the Triangle

This is very important. You must label the sides and angles properly so that the letters for the sides and angles correspond with each other. Use <u>lower case letters</u> for the <u>sides</u> and <u>capitals</u> for the <u>angles</u>.

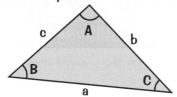

Remember, <u>side 'a' is opposite angle A</u> etc.

It doesn't matter which sides you decide to call a, b, and c, just as long as the angles are then labelled properly.

Three Formulas to Learn:

> These formulas will be on the formula sheet in the exam.

The Sine Rule

$$\frac{a}{\sin A} = \frac{b}{\sin B} = \frac{c}{\sin C}$$

You don't use the whole thing with both '=' signs of course, so it's not half as bad as it looks — you just <u>choose the two bits</u> that you want:

e.g. $\dfrac{b}{\sin B} = \dfrac{c}{\sin C}$ or $\dfrac{a}{\sin A} = \dfrac{b}{\sin B}$

The Cosine Rule

The 'normal' form is...

$$a^2 = b^2 + c^2 - 2bc \cos A$$

...or this form, which is good for finding an angle (you get it by rearranging the 'normal' version):

or $\cos A = \dfrac{b^2 + c^2 - a^2}{2bc}$

Area of the Triangle

This formula comes in handy when you know <u>two sides</u> and the <u>angle between them</u>:

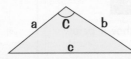

$$\text{Area of triangle} = \tfrac{1}{2} ab \sin C$$

> Of course, you already know a simple formula for calculating the area using the base length and height (see p.41). The formula here is for when you don't know those values.

EXAMPLE: Find the area of the shaded segment in the diagram on the right.

The area of the <u>segment</u> is the <u>difference</u> between the area of the <u>sector</u> and the area of the <u>triangle</u>.

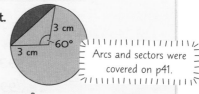

> Arcs and sectors were covered on p41.

1 Area of sector $= \dfrac{x}{360°}\pi r^2 = \dfrac{60°}{360°} \times \pi \times 3^2 = 4.7123...$

2 Area of triangle $= \tfrac{1}{2} ab \sin x = \tfrac{1}{2} \times 3 \times 3 \times \sin 60° = 3.8971...$

3 Area of segment $= 4.7123... - 3.8971...$

$= 0.81527...$

$= 0.815 \text{ cm}^2$ (3 s.f.)

Tri angles — go on, you might like them...

You need to learn these formulas and make sure you know how to use them. Here's an area question to have a go at, and fear not — you'll get your chance to tackle some sine and cosine rule problems on the next page...

Q1 Triangle FGH has FG = 9 cm, FH = 12 cm and angle GFH = 37°. Find its area, giving your answer correct to 3 significant figures.

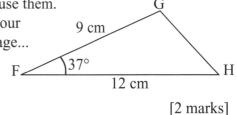

[2 marks]

The Sine and Cosine Rules

There are four main question types where the <u>sine</u> and <u>cosine</u> rules would be applied. So learn the exact details of these four examples and you'll be laughing. WARNING: if you laugh too much people will think you're crazy.

The Four Examples

TWO ANGLES given plus ANY SIDE — SINE RULE needed.

Find the length of AB for the triangle below.

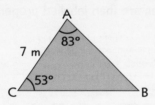

1) Don't forget the obvious... $B = 180° - 83° - 53° = 44°$

2) Put the <u>numbers</u> into the <u>sine rule</u>. $\dfrac{b}{\sin B} = \dfrac{c}{\sin C} \Rightarrow \dfrac{7}{\sin 44°} = \dfrac{c}{\sin 53°}$

3) <u>Rearrange</u> to find c. $\Rightarrow c = \dfrac{7 \times \sin 53°}{\sin 44°} = 8.05\,\text{m (3 s.f.)}$

2 **TWO SIDES given plus an ANGLE NOT ENCLOSED by them — SINE RULE needed.**

Find angle ABC for the triangle shown below.

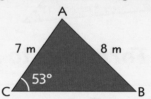

1) Put the <u>numbers</u> into the <u>sine rule</u>. $\dfrac{b}{\sin B} = \dfrac{c}{\sin C} \Rightarrow \dfrac{7}{\sin B} = \dfrac{8}{\sin 53°}$

2) <u>Rearrange</u> to find sin B. $\Rightarrow \sin B = \dfrac{7 \times \sin 53°}{8} = 0.6988...$

3) Find the <u>inverse</u>. $\Rightarrow B = \sin^{-1}(0.6988...) = 44.3°\,(1\,\text{d.p.})$

3 **TWO SIDES given plus the ANGLE ENCLOSED by them — COSINE RULE needed.**

Find the length CB for the triangle shown below.

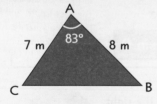

1) Put the <u>numbers</u> into the <u>cosine rule</u>.
$a^2 = b^2 + c^2 - 2bc \cos A$
$= 7^2 + 8^2 - 2 \times 7 \times 8 \times \cos 83°$
$= 99.3506...$

2) Take <u>square roots</u> to find a.
$a = \sqrt{99.3506...}$
$= 9.97\,\text{m (3 s.f.)}$

You might come across a triangle that isn't labelled ABC — just <u>relabel it</u> yourself to match the sine and cosine rules.

4 **ALL THREE SIDES given but NO ANGLES — COSINE RULE needed.**

Find angle CAB for the triangle shown.

1) Use this version of the <u>cosine rule</u>. $\cos A = \dfrac{b^2 + c^2 - a^2}{2bc}$

2) <u>Put in</u> the <u>numbers</u>. $= \dfrac{49 + 64 - 100}{2 \times 7 \times 8}$

3) <u>Take the inverse</u> to find A. $= \dfrac{13}{112} = 0.11607...$
$\Rightarrow A = \cos^{-1}(0.11607...)$
$= 83.3°\,(1\,\text{d.p.})$

4 examples + 3 formulas + 2 rules = 1 trigonometric genius...

You need to get really good at spotting which of the four methods to use, so try these questions.

Q1 Find the length of side AB in triangle ABC.

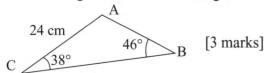

24 cm, A, 46°, B, 38°, C   [3 marks]

Q2 Find the size of angle RPQ in triangle PQR.

P, 15 m, R, 9 m, Q, 13 m   [3 marks]

Trigonometry with Bearings

Bearings. They'll be useful next time you're off sailing. Or in your Maths exam.

Bearings *Always Go* Clockwise *from North*

To find or plot a bearing you must remember <u>the three key words</u>:

1) 'FROM'   <u>Find the word 'FROM' in the question</u>, and put your pencil on the diagram at the point you are going '<u>from</u>'.

2) NORTH LINE   At the point you are going <u>FROM</u>, <u>draw in a NORTH LINE</u>. (There'll often be one drawn for you in exam questions.)

3) CLOCKWISE   Now draw in the angle CLOCKWISE <u>from the north line to the line joining the two points</u>. This angle is the required bearing.

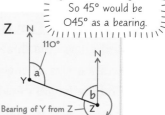

The bearing of A from B

Bearings are always given as three figures. So 45° would be 045° as a bearing.

EXAMPLE: The bearing of Z from Y is 110°. Find the bearing of Y from Z.

See page 36 for allied angles.

First sketch a diagram so you can see what's going on.
Angles a and b are <u>allied</u>, so they add up to <u>180°</u>.
Angle b = 180° − 110° = 70°
So bearing of Y from Z = 360° − 70° = 290°.

Bearing of Y from Z

If You See Bearings, You'll Probably Need Trig

Bearings and trig are both to do with <u>angles</u>, so it's no shock they go together like spaghetti and meatballs.

You're probably going to need the <u>sine</u> or <u>cosine rule</u> if one of these questions comes up in the exam, so flip back to page **59** and remind yourself about them before we get started.

EXAMPLE: An island chain consists of three islands: Sunland, Torrenta and Raynami. Sunland is 7 km due West of Raynami. Torrenta is 12 km away from Raynami on a bearing of 163°. This is shown in the diagram below.

Find: a) the distance between Sunland and Torrenta,
        b) the bearing on which you would travel from Torrenta to Sunland.

First <u>convert</u> the bearings into angles that are in the <u>triangle</u>.

$$90° + 163° + S\widehat{R}T = 360° \Rightarrow S\widehat{R}T = 107°$$

You're given <u>two sides</u> and the <u>angle enclosed</u> by them so use the <u>cosine rule</u>.

a) $ST^2 = SR^2 + RT^2 - 2(SR)(RT)\cos S\widehat{R}T$
$= 7^2 + 12^2 - 2 \times 7 \times 12 \cos 107°$
$= 193 - 168 \cos 107° = 242.1184...$
$ST = \sqrt{242.1184...} = 15.56015... = 15.6$ km (1 d.p.)

You now have <u>two sides</u> and an <u>angle not enclosed</u> by them so use the <u>sine rule</u> to find $R\widehat{T}S$.

b) $\dfrac{SR}{\sin R\widehat{T}S} = \dfrac{ST}{\sin S\widehat{R}T} \Rightarrow \sin R\widehat{T}S = \dfrac{SR \sin S\widehat{R}T}{ST} = \dfrac{7 \sin 107°}{15.56015...} = 0.43020...$

$\Rightarrow R\widehat{T}S = \sin^{-1}(0.43020...) = 25.480...°$

Use <u>allied angles</u> to find the angle between the <u>North line</u> and <u>RT</u>, then subtract from 360° to get the <u>clockwise bearing</u>.

The angle between the North line at T and RT is 180° − 163° = 17°.

So the bearing from T to S is
360° − 17° − 25.480...° = 317.519...° = 318°

You could have used the <u>cosine rule</u> instead in b) since you know <u>three sides</u>.

Please bear with me while I figure out where we are...

Never forget — bearings are always measured <u>clockwise</u> from <u>North</u>. Now try this Practice Question:

Q1   a)   A ship sails 12 km on a bearing of 050°, then 20 km on a bearing of 100°. It then sails directly back to its starting position. Calculate this distance to 1 d.p.   **[4 marks]**

     b)   Find the bearing on which the ship sails on its way back to its starting position.   **[3 marks]**

Revision Questions for Section Four

Lots of <u>formulas</u> to learn in <u>Section Four</u> — have a go at this page to check you've got them <u>sorted</u>.

- Try these questions and <u>tick off each one</u> when you <u>get it right</u>.
- When you've done <u>all the questions</u> for a topic and are <u>completely happy</u> with it, tick off the topic.

<u>Trigonometric Graphs (p52-54)</u> ☑

1) Sketch the graphs of sin x, cos x and tan x for $0° \leq x \leq 360°$, labelling all the max/min/zero/undefined points.

2) What is the period and amplitude of sin x?

3) On separate axes, sketch the following graphs for $-360° \leq x \leq 360°$:
   a) $y = 5 \sin x$ b) $y = \cos x - 7$ c) $y = \sin(3x)$ d) $y = \cos(x + 180°)$

4) Sketch the graph of sin x following a translation by a phase angle of $60°$ between $0° \leq x \leq 360°$.

<u>Sin, Cos and Tan (p55-56)</u> ☑

5) Write down the three basic trigonometry formulas.

6) Find the size of angle x in triangle ABC to 1 d.p. ⟹

7) Find the length of side XZ in triangle XYZ. ⟹

8) If cos x = 0.9, find all the possible values of x in the interval $0° \leq x \leq 360°$.

9) Solve $\sin x = -\frac{2}{3}$ for $0° \leq x \leq 360°$.

10) Without using your calculator, put the values sin 50°, sin 270° and sin 315° in ascending order.

<u>Trig Equations and Identities (p57-58)</u> ☑

11) Solve $3 \tan x - 3 = 5$ for $0° \leq x \leq 360°$.

12) Find where the graph of $y = 5 \sin x + 2$ intersects the x-axis in the range $0° \leq x \leq 360°$.

13) What is tan x in terms of sin x and cos x?

14) What is $\cos^2 x$ in terms of $\sin^2 x$?

15) Prove that $1 + \tan^2 x = \frac{1}{\cos^2 x}$.

16) Show that $\frac{\sin^4 x + \sin^2 x \cos^2 x}{-\sin^2 x} \equiv -1$.

17) Simplify: $(\sin y + \cos y)^2 + (\cos y - \sin y)^2$.

<u>The Sine Rule, Cosine Rule and Bearings (p59-61)</u> ☑

18) Write down the sine and cosine rules and the formula (involving sin) for the area of any triangle.

19) List the 4 different types of sine/cosine rule questions and which rule you need for each.

20) Triangle JKL has side JK = 7 cm, side JL = 11 cm and angle JLK = 32°. Find angle JKL.

21) In triangle FGH side FH = 8 cm, side GH = 9 cm and angle FHG = 47°. Find the length of side FG.

22) Triangle PQR has side PQ = 12 cm, side QR = 9 cm and angle PQR = 63°. Find its area.

23) WXYZ is a quadrilateral.
   a) Find the length of side XY to 3 s.f.
   b) Find the area of the quadrilateral to 3 s.f.

24) A ship sails due South from Port F to Port G. It then sails on a bearing of 085° to Port H. Its distance from Port F is 375 km and the bearing from Port F to Port H is 115°.
   a) Find the bearing on which the ship would have to sail to return directly to Port F.
   b) (i) How far is Port G from Port F?
      (ii) How far is Port G from Port H?

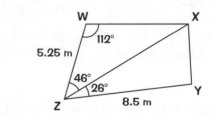

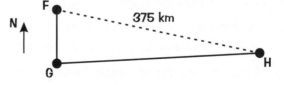

Mean, Median, Mode and Range

Mean, median and mode are all types of average. The range tells you about the spread of the data.
You should be familiar with these measures — but here's a recap to make sure you've got them sussed.

The Four Definitions

> MODE = MOST common
>
> MEDIAN = MIDDLE value (when values are in order of size)
>
> MEAN = TOTAL of items ÷ NUMBER of items
>
> RANGE = Difference between highest and lowest

REMEMBER:

Mode = most (emphasise the 'mo' in each when you say them)

Median = mid (emphasise the m*d in each when you say them)

Mean is just the average, but it's mean 'cos you have to work it out.

The Golden Rule

There's one vital step for finding the median that lots of people forget:

> Always REARRANGE the data in ASCENDING ORDER

(and check you have the same number of entries!)

You absolutely must do this when finding the median,
but it's also really useful for working out the mode too.

EXAMPLE: Find the median, mode, mean, and range of these numbers:

2, 5, 3, 2, 6, −4, 0, 9, −3, 1, 6, 3, −2, 3

Check that you still have the same number of entries after you've rearranged them.

The **MEDIAN** is the middle value (when they're arranged in order of size)
— so first, rearrange the numbers.

When there are two middle numbers, the median is halfway between the two.

−4, −3, −2, 0, 1, 2, (2, 3) 3, 3, 5, 6, 6, 9

← seven numbers this side ↑ seven numbers this side →

Median = 2.5

An even number of values means there will be two middle numbers.

MODE (or modal value) is the most common value. ⟶ Mode = 3

Data sets can have more than one mode.

$$\text{MEAN} = \frac{\text{total of items}}{\text{number of items}} \longrightarrow \frac{-4-3-2+0+1+2+2+3+3+3+5+6+6+9}{14}$$

$$= 31 \div 14 = 2.214... = 2.21 \text{ (3 s.f.)}$$

RANGE = distance from lowest to highest value, i.e. from −4 up to 9. ⟶ 9 − (−4) = 13

Choose the Best Average

The mean, median and mode
all have their advantages
and disadvantages:

	Advantages	Disadvantages
Mean	Uses all the data. Usually most representative.	Isn't always a data value. May be distorted by extreme data values.
Median	Easy to find in ordered data. Not distorted by extreme data values.	Isn't always a data value. Not always a good representation of the data.
Mode	Easy to find in tallied data. Always a data value.	Sometimes there's more than one. Not always a good representation of the data.

Strike a pose, there's nothing to it — mode...

Learn the four definitions and the extra step you have to do to find the median, then give this a go...

Q1   Find the mean, median, mode and range for the set of data below:

1, 3, 14, −5, 6, −12, 18, 7, 23, 10, −5, −14, 0, 25, 8.   [4 marks]

Quartiles and Standard Deviation

Exciting news folks... there are more ways to measure <u>how spread out</u> a set of data is. There's the <u>interquartile range</u>, the <u>semi-interquartile range</u> (pleasingly similar) and <u>standard deviation</u> (totally different).

Quartiles Divide the Data into Four Equal Groups

1) The quartiles are the <u>lower quartile</u> Q_1, the <u>median</u> Q_2 and the <u>upper quartile</u> Q_3.

2) If you put the data in <u>ascending order</u>, the quartiles are <u>25%</u> (¼), <u>50%</u> (½) and <u>75%</u> (¾) of the way through the list. The <u>median</u> (Q_2) splits the data values into two equal groups. To find Q_1, find the <u>middle value</u> of the <u>lower</u> group, and to find Q_3, find the <u>middle value</u> of the <u>upper</u> group. As for the median, if there are <u>two middle values</u>, you'll need to find the average.

3) The <u>INTERQUARTILE RANGE</u> (IQR) is the <u>difference</u> between the <u>upper quartile</u> and the <u>lower quartile</u> — it tells you the spread of the <u>middle 50%</u> of values.

4) The <u>SEMI-INTERQUARTILE RANGE</u> (SIQR) is just <u>half of the IQR</u>, so that's: $\dfrac{Q_3 - Q_1}{2}$

EXAMPLE: Here are the ages, in months, of a number of fine cheeses: 7, 12, 5, 4, 3, 9, 5, 11, 7, 5, 7
Find the median and semi-interquartile range of the ages.

<u>Check</u> you've got the <u>right number</u> of values — 11 ✓

1) Put the data in <u>order of size</u>. ⟶ 3, 4, 5, 5, 5, 7, 7, 7, 9, 11, 12

2) Find the median Q_2 3, 4, 5, 5, 5, ⑦ 7, 7, 9, 11, 12 — the middle value is 7 months

3) Find Q_1 (3, 4, ⑤ 5, 5,) 7, (7, 7, 9, 11, 12) — the middle of the lower group is 5

4) Find Q_3 (3, 4, 5, 5, 5,) 7, (7, 7, ⑨ 11, 12) — the middle of the upper group is 9

5) <u>Subtract</u> Q_1 from Q_3 and <u>divide</u> by 2.   Semi-interquartile range $= \dfrac{Q_3 - Q_1}{2} = \dfrac{9-5}{2} = 2$ months

There are <u>different methods</u> for finding quartiles — you might have learnt a different one to the example above.
E.g. you might have used the formulas (n + 1)/4 and 3(n + 1)/4 to find the positions of Q_1 and Q_3.

Standard Deviation Measures Spread from the Mean

The <u>standard deviation</u> tells you how <u>spread out</u> from the <u>mean</u> the values are. The <u>SMALLER</u> it is, the <u>closer</u> the data is to the <u>mean</u>. To calculate standard deviation, you use <u>all</u> the values in the data set — this can make it <u>more useful</u> than other measures of spread. However, it is affected by <u>extreme values</u>.

The <u>formula</u> can be written in <u>two different ways</u> — use which you find <u>easiest</u>.
The formula to find the <u>standard deviation</u> (s) of a set of <u>n</u> data values, x_1, x_2, ..., x_n, with <u>mean</u> $\bar{x}$ is:

This symbol means 'sum' — you <u>add up</u> the values of $(x - \bar{x})^2$.

or

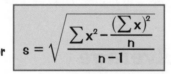

Good news — these formulas will be <u>given</u> to you in the exam... More good news — they're <u>not as bad as they look</u> once you break them down into smaller steps.

EXAMPLE: Calculate the standard deviation of this data: 22, 20, 25, 18, 19.

1) First find the <u>mean</u>:   Mean $= \bar{x} = \dfrac{22 + 20 + 25 + 18 + 19}{5} = 20.8$

2) <u>Make a table</u> to list the values you need to find. I'm using the <u>first</u> formula for s, so need columns for x, $(x - \bar{x})$ and $(x - \bar{x})^2$:

3) Now you're ready to <u>substitute</u> into the formula for <u>s</u>:

$$s = \sqrt{\dfrac{\sum (x - \bar{x})^2}{n-1}} = \sqrt{\dfrac{30.8}{5-1}}$$

$$= 2.774... = 2.77 \ (2 \text{ d.p.})$$

Try the 2nd formula for yourself — you'll need columns for x and x^2.

x	$(x - \bar{x})$	$(x - \bar{x})^2$
22	1.2	1.44
20	−0.8	0.64
25	4.2	17.64
18	−2.8	7.84
19	−1.8	3.24
Total		30.8

Comparing Data Sets

All that work you've done on <u>averages and spread</u> will come in very handy here...

Compare Data Using Averages and Spread

1 <u>AVERAGES</u> — <u>MEAN</u>, <u>MEDIAN</u> or <u>MODE</u> — say which data set has the <u>higher/lower</u> value and <u>what that means</u> in the context of the data. Remember, each measure has its <u>pros and cons</u> (see p.63).

2 <u>SPREAD</u> — <u>RANGE</u>, <u>INTERQUARTILE RANGE</u>, <u>SEMI-INTERQUARTILE RANGE</u> or <u>STANDARD DEVIATION</u>.

1) Say which data set has the <u>larger/smaller</u> value. A <u>larger spread</u> means the values are <u>less consistent</u> or there is <u>more variation</u> in the data.

2) Remember that the <u>range</u> and <u>standard deviation</u> can both be affected by <u>extreme</u> values, and <u>standard deviation</u> is the only measure that uses <u>all</u> the data values.

Exam questions might ask you to <u>calculate measures</u>, and then to <u>use them</u> to make <u>comparisons</u>.

EXAMPLE:

A meteorologist records the rainfall (to the nearest mm) in six towns on a particular day in March. Here is his data: 2, 0, 5, 14, 10, 17.

a) Calculate the mean and standard deviation of these values.

1) $\underline{\text{Mean}} = \frac{\text{total of items}}{\text{number of items}} \longrightarrow \text{Mean} = \bar{x} = \frac{2+0+5+14+10+17}{6} = \frac{48}{6} = 8 \text{ mm}$

2) For the <u>standard deviation</u>, <u>make a table</u> to list the values you need to find. I'm using the <u>first formula for s</u> given on the previous page. $\longrightarrow$

3) Now <u>substitute</u> into the formula: $\longrightarrow$ $s = \sqrt{\dfrac{\sum(x-\bar{x})^2}{n-1}} = \sqrt{\dfrac{230}{6-1}}$

$= 6.782... = 6.78 \text{ mm (2 d.p.)}$

x	$(x-\bar{x})$	$(x-\bar{x})^2$
2	−6	36
0	−8	64
5	−3	9
14	6	36
10	2	4
17	9	81
		230

b) Rainfall data was recorded for the six towns on a day in June. This data has a mean of 3.5 mm and a standard deviation of 2 mm. Make two valid comparisons between the March data and the June data.

1) Use the <u>mean</u>: The June rainfall values are lower on average, since the mean rainfall is lower.

2) Use the <u>standard deviation</u>: There is less variation in the June rainfall values, since the standard deviation is smaller.

EXAMPLE:

Fran and Maya both record the length of time they have to queue at the supermarket. Fran's queuing times have a median of 7.2 minutes and a semi-interquartile range of 3.8 minutes. Maya's queuing times have a median of 9.4 minutes and a semi-interquartile range of 1.1 minutes. Make two valid comparisons between Fran's and Maya's queuing times.

Compare <u>median</u> and <u>SIQR</u> values: Fran's queuing times are shorter on average, since her median queuing time is lower. Maya's queuing times are more consistent, since her semi-interquartile range is smaller.

Maths-up your home with our standard inter-floortile range...

Make sure you're confident with the measures of average and spread, then give this question a whirl:

Q1 a) A sample of grubs has the following lengths (in cm): 3.0, 1.6, 1.4, 2.2, 0.7, 1.1, 2.6
        Find the median length and the semi-interquartile range. [3 marks]

    b) A different sample of grubs has a median length of 1.8 cm and a semi-interquartile
        range of 0.9 cm. Compare the lengths of the two samples of grubs. [2 marks]

Scattergraphs

A <u>scattergraph</u> tells you <u>how closely</u> two things are <u>related</u> — the fancy word is <u>CORRELATION</u>.

Scattergraphs Show Correlation

1) If you can draw a <u>line of best fit</u> pretty close to <u>most</u> of your data points, the two things are <u>correlated</u>. If the points are <u>randomly scattered</u>, and you <u>can't draw</u> a line of best fit, then there's <u>no correlation</u>.

2) <u>Strong correlation</u> is when your points make a <u>fairly straight line</u> — this means the two things are <u>closely related</u> to each other. <u>Weak correlation</u> is when your points <u>don't line up</u> quite so nicely, but you can still draw a line of best fit through them.

3) If the points form a line sloping <u>uphill</u> from left to right, then there is <u>positive correlation</u> — both things increase or decrease <u>together</u>. If the line slopes <u>downhill</u> from left to right, then there is <u>negative correlation</u> — as one thing <u>increases</u> the other <u>decreases</u>.

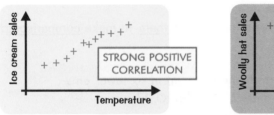
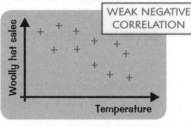
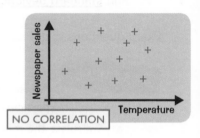

4) <u>BE CAREFUL</u> with <u>correlation</u> — if two things are correlated it <u>doesn't mean</u> that one causes the other. There could be a third factor affecting both, or it could just be a coincidence.

Drawing a Line of Best Fit Shows the Trend

1) A <u>line of best fit</u> is a straight line through the <u>middle</u> of your data points — with roughly the <u>same number of points</u> on either side of the line.

2) You can use the line of best fit to see the <u>trend</u> in the data and to <u>make estimates</u> — there's lots more on estimating on the next page.

3) Watch out for <u>outliers</u> — data points that <u>don't fit the general pattern</u>. These might be errors, but aren't necessarily. Outliers can <u>drag</u> your <u>line of best fit</u> away from the other values, so it's best to <u>ignore</u> them when you're drawing the line.

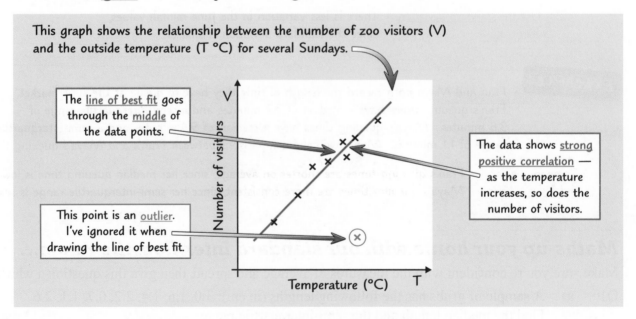

This graph shows the relationship between the number of zoo visitors (V) and the outside temperature (T °C) for several Sundays.

The <u>line of best fit</u> goes through the <u>middle</u> of the data points.

The data shows <u>strong positive correlation</u> — as the temperature increases, so does the number of visitors.

This point is an <u>outlier</u>. I've ignored it when drawing the line of best fit.

So that's the basics of scattergraphs covered — now onto the <u>good stuff</u>...

Scattergraphs

... and by good stuff I mean finding the equation of your line of best fit and making predictions.

Find the Equation of a Line of Best Fit

1) You can describe the relationship between your two sets of data by finding the equation of your line of best fit.
2) To find the equation of a straight line, use the method from p.23.

EXAMPLE: Below is the graph from the previous page, showing the relationship between the number of zoo visitors (V) and the outside temperature (T °C) for several Sundays.

A line of best fit is shown — Point A represents a Sunday where the zoo had 1800 visitors and the outside temperature was 10 °C and Point B represents a Sunday where the zoo had 3300 visitors and the outside temperature was 20 °C.

Find the equation of the line of best fit in terms of T and V. Give your answer in its simplest form.

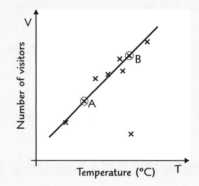

1) Use the points A and B to find the gradient:

$$m = \frac{\text{change in V}}{\text{change in T}} = \frac{3300 - 1800}{20 - 10} = \frac{1500}{10} = 150$$

2) Substitute into the equation of a straight line for T and V:

$m = 150$ and $(a, b) = (10, 1800)$
$V - b = m(T - a)$, so $V - 1800 = 150(T - 10)$
$V - 1800 = 150T - 1500$
$V = 150T + 300$

Use a Line of Best Fit to Make Predictions

You can use the equation of your line of best fit to make estimates. Predicting a value within the range of data you have (called interpolation) should be fairly reliable, since you can see the pattern within this range. Predicting a value outside the range of data (called extrapolation) might be unreliable, since you're just assuming the pattern continues.

EXAMPLE: Use the equation of the line from the example above to estimate the number of visitors the zoo could expect on a Sunday with an outside temperature of 15 °C.

Just substitute T = 15 into the equation of the line:
$V = 150T + 300$
$V = 150 \times 15 + 300 = 2550$
So the zoo could expect 2550 visitors.

Relax and take a trip down Correlation Street...

Q1 Joe measures his average speed (S mph) on runs of different length (L miles). This scattergraph shows the relationship between S and L. A line of best fit with points A = (3, 6.5) and B = (8, 5) is shown.

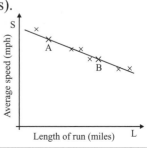

a) Find the equation of the line of best fit in terms of L and S. Give the equation in its simplest form. [3 marks]

b) Use your equation to estimate Joe's average speed for a 4-mile run. Show your working. [1 mark]

Revision Questions for Section Five

Here's the inevitable list of straight-down-the-middle questions to test how much you know.

- Try these questions and <u>tick off each one</u> when you <u>get it right</u>.
- When you've done <u>all the questions</u> for a topic and are <u>completely happy</u> with it, tick off the topic.

Averages and Spread (p63-64) ☑

1) Write down the definitions for the mode, median, mean and range. ☐

2) Find the mode, median, mean and range of this data: 2, 8, 11, 15, 22, 24, 27, 30, 31, 31, 41 ☐

3) Below are the prices, in pence per kilogram, of eight varieties of potato on sale at a supermarket:
62, 100, 74, 112, 85, 132, 55, 98
Calculate: a) the median price   b) the mean price ☐

4) For the data 18, 35, 27, 62, 47, find:
a) The median, the lower quartile and the upper quartile.
b) The interquartile range.
c) The semi-interquartile range. ☐

5) Aileen recorded her scores for her last ten rounds of golf: 74, 75, 72, 72, 68, 73, 71, 70, 68, 67.
Find the semi-interquartile range of her scores. ☐

6) The standard deviation of 3, 8 and 10 is equal to $\sqrt{b}$. Work out the value of b. ☐

7) Here are ten data values: 2, 3, 3, 3, 4, 5, 5, 7, 8, 10.
The standard deviation of these data values can be written as $\frac{c\sqrt{d}}{3}$ in its simplest form.
Calculate the values of c and d. ☐

Comparing Data Sets (p65) ☑

8) Saleem works in customer services. He records the number of queries he deals with each day
for a period of 5 days: 18, 25, 32, 21, 29.
a) Calculate the mean and standard deviation of his numbers of queries.
b) Jeff recorded the number of queries he dealt with over the same 5-day period. His mean number
of queries was 19 and the standard deviation was 3.9. Make two valid comparisons between
the number of queries Saleem dealt with and the number of queries Jeff dealt with. ☐

9) The table opposite summarises the
time it took Henry to travel to work
in summer and winter last year.

	Summer (time in mins)	Winter (time in mins)
Median	29	26
Lower quartile	20	19
Upper quartile	33	40

a) Find the semi-interquartile range for the
summer times and the winter times.
b) Make two valid comparisons between the summer and winter journey times. ☐

Scattergraphs (p66-67) ☑

10) Sketch scattergraphs to show:
a) weak positive correlation,   b) strong negative correlation,   c) no correlation ☐

11) The students in a class complete a Maths test and a Physics test.
The graph opposite shows the relationship between the students'
Maths marks and Physics marks. Point A shows a student who
scored 20 in Maths and 15 in Physics, and point B shows a student
who scored 70 in Maths and 60 in Physics.
Find the equation of the line of best fit in terms of M and P. ☐

12) Use the equation you found in Q11 to estimate the Physics mark
for a student who scored 40 in the Maths test. ☐

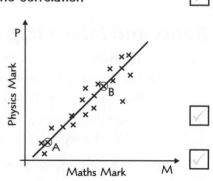

Reasoning Skills

Reasoning skills are all about how you tackle a mathematical problem and explain the answer.
You'll have to use reasoning skills on both exam papers, so it's a good idea to know what you need to do.

There are Two Main Types of Reasoning Questions...

1) For some questions, it's <u>obvious</u> what you have to do — e.g. 'solve the equation $x^2 + 5x + 6 = 0$'
   is clearly a question on <u>quadratic equations</u>, so solve it using the usual methods (see p.24-27).

2) However, in other questions, it's <u>not obvious</u> what you have to do — you're given some <u>information</u>,
   and have to work out what <u>methods</u> to use to answer the question. These questions are designed to
   assess how you approach an <u>unfamiliar problem</u> — they test your <u>reasoning skills</u>.

3) Reasoning questions come in <u>two different forms</u> —
   in both cases, you have to work out what maths to do <u>for yourself</u>.

Questions With a Real-Life Context

1) If questions have a <u>real-life context</u>, the information you need might be <u>hidden</u> in all the wordiness.
   You need to read through the question and work out which bits are <u>relevant</u> to the maths,
   and which bits are just <u>setting the scene</u>.

2) Once you've worked this out, decide which <u>method(s)</u> you need to use to answer the question.
   After doing all your <u>calculations</u>, make sure you <u>link</u> your answer back to the <u>original context</u>.

3) It can be pretty obvious what maths you need to use, even with a real-life context —
   <u>scientific notation</u> and <u>simultaneous equations</u> are often given in context.
   Sometimes it's <u>not</u> that obvious though — which leads us nicely onto...

Problem-Solving Questions

> Sometimes questions will be a mixture of both —
> i.e. problem-solving questions set in a real-life context.

1) In <u>problem-solving questions</u>, you'll be given a load of <u>mathematical information</u>
   (sometimes including <u>diagrams</u>) and asked to '<u>calculate</u>' or '<u>find</u>' a certain value.
   It's then up to you to come up with a <u>strategy</u> to answer the question.

2) You won't be given any <u>guidance</u> for what method to use — you have work it out for yourself.

3) There are often a couple of <u>different ways</u> you could answer the question — and you'll get the
   marks whichever way you do it, as long as you get the <u>answer</u> right and <u>show your working</u> clearly.

Here are Some Useful Tips for Reasoning Questions

Unfortunately, there's <u>no</u> one set method for answering reasoning questions — they can be on anything
the examiners fancy, so will involve <u>different bits</u> of maths. These <u>tips</u> should help you get started though.

- <u>Read the question</u> two or three times and work out what you're <u>trying to find</u>.
- Write down what you <u>know</u> — pick out any <u>numbers</u> given in the question, and add <u>labels</u> to
  diagrams if you can. If you're not given a diagram, it's often a good idea to <u>sketch one yourself</u>.
- See if anything <u>jumps out</u> at you — for example, <u>right-angled triangles</u> might mean you need to
  use <u>Pythagoras</u> or <u>trigonometry</u>, or <u>squared terms</u> might mean you're working with a <u>quadratic</u>.
- <u>Don't rush</u> into a problem-solving question — <u>take your time</u> and <u>think it through</u> first.
  Make sure you have an <u>idea</u> of what you're going to do before diving in.
- <u>Show all your working</u> — these questions can be worth <u>4 or 5 marks</u>, so you'll get
  some marks for your <u>strategy</u> and <u>reasoning</u> even if you get the final answer <u>wrong</u>.
- Make sure your answer is <u>sensible</u> — look back at the <u>original question</u>
  and check that it seems <u>reasonable</u>.

There's an <u>example</u> of a reasoning question coming up on the <u>next page</u>.

Reasoning Skills — Worked Example

Now you know what reasoning questions are and how to tackle them, it's time to see one in the wild...

Put it into Practice With a Worked Example

The best way to get to grips with reasoning questions is to see them <u>in action</u> — so here's a <u>worked example</u> to show you how it's done. Remember, all reasoning questions are <u>different</u> — but you can apply the <u>same skills</u> to tackle them.

Natalie is making a Christmas card with a snowman design. To make the shape of the snowman, she uses two circles, one of radius 4 cm and one of radius 3 cm. She intersects the circles, as shown below. The chord where the two circles meet has length 4.6 cm. Find h, the height of the snowman. Give your answer to 3 significant figures.

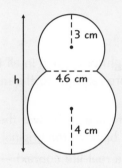

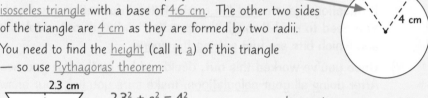

<u>Split the shape up</u> and deal with each bit separately:

On the bottom part of the shape, you can create an <u>isosceles triangle</u> with a base of <u>4.6 cm</u>. The other two sides of the triangle are <u>4 cm</u> as they are formed by two radii.

You need to find the <u>height</u> (call it <u>a</u>) of this triangle — so use <u>Pythagoras' theorem</u>:

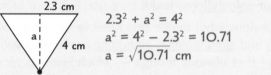

$$2.3^2 + a^2 = 4^2$$
$$a^2 = 4^2 - 2.3^2 = 10.71$$
$$a = \sqrt{10.71}\ \text{cm}$$

Leave the square root in for now — if you round too early, you'll lose accuracy.

So the height of this part of the shape is the <u>radius</u> plus the height of the <u>triangle</u>: $(4 + \sqrt{10.71})$ cm

Now repeat for the top part of the shape:

This time, you get an isosceles triangle with base <u>4.6 cm</u> and sides of length <u>3 cm</u>. Now find its <u>height</u> (call it <u>b</u>):

$$2.3^2 + b^2 = 3^2$$
$$b^2 = 3^2 - 2.3^2 = 3.71$$
$$b = \sqrt{3.71}\ \text{cm}$$

So the height of this part of the shape is: $(3 + \sqrt{3.71})$ cm

The final step is to <u>add up</u> the heights of each bit of the shape to find h:

$$h = (4 + \sqrt{10.71}) + (3 + \sqrt{3.71}) = 12.1987... = 12.2\ \text{cm (3 s.f.)}$$

So there you have it. In this example, the <u>maths itself</u> wasn't too bad (just a bit of Pythagoras), but if you hadn't <u>realised</u> that you needed to use Pythagoras, you'd have been stumped.

Watch out for questions that are a bit <u>sneaky</u> — here, you might have thought that you needed to use the formulas for arcs and sectors because the question involved <u>circles</u> — but that would have wasted time.

Well, I think you're just being unreasonable...

The main thing to remember with problem-solving questions is: <u>don't panic</u>. Even if you don't know what to do, try writing down everything you know (or can find) and see where you are.

Q1 A regular octagon is drawn inside a circle, so that the vertices of the octagon just touch the circumference of the circle, as shown in the diagram. The radius of the circle is 4 cm. Find the area between the octagon and the circle (the shaded region of the diagram). Give your answer to 2 s.f. [5 marks]

Exam Tips

Following the tips below will help you get as many marks as possible in your exams — but they're no use if you haven't <u>learnt the stuff</u> in the first place. So revise well and do <u>as many</u> practice questions as you can.

Exam Stuff

1) You will have <u>two</u> exams — one <u>non-calculator</u> exam and one <u>calculator</u> exam.

2) The non-calculator exam is <u>1 hr 15 mins</u> long and worth <u>50 marks</u>.

3) The calculator exam is <u>1 hr 50 mins</u> long and worth <u>60 marks</u>.

4) Timings in the exams are really important, so here's a quick guide...

- You should spend roughly 1-1.5 <u>minutes per mark</u> working on each question (i.e. 2 marks = 2-3 minutes).
- Then, if you've got any <u>time left</u> at the end of the exams, <u>check</u> back through your answers and make sure you haven't made any silly mistakes. <u>Don't just</u> stare at that hottie in front.
- If you're totally, hopelessly stuck on a question, just <u>leave it</u> and <u>move on</u> to the next one. You can always <u>go back</u> to it at the end if you've got enough time.

There are a Few Golden Rules

1) ALWAYS, ALWAYS, ALWAYS MAKE SURE YOU <u>READ THE QUESTION PROPERLY</u>.
   For example, if the question asks you to give your answer in metres, don't give it in centimetres.

2) SHOW <u>EACH STEP IN YOUR WORKING</u>.
   You're less likely to make a mistake if you write things out in stages. And even if your final answer's wrong, you'll probably pick up some marks if the examiner sees that your method is right.

3) CHECK THAT YOUR ANSWER IS <u>SENSIBLE</u>.
   Worked out an angle of 450° or 0.045° in a triangle? You've probably gone wrong somewhere...

4) MAKE SURE YOU GIVE YOUR ANSWER TO THE <u>RIGHT DEGREE OF ACCURACY</u>.
   The question might ask you to round to a certain number of significant figures or decimal places. So make sure you do just that, otherwise you'll almost certainly lose marks.

5) LOOK AT THE <u>NUMBER OF MARKS</u> A QUESTION IS WORTH.
   If a question's worth 2 or more marks, you're not going to get them all for just writing down the final answer — you're going to have to show your working.

6) WRITE YOUR ANSWERS AS <u>CLEARLY AS YOU CAN</u>.
   If the examiner can't read your answer you won't get any marks, even if it's right.

Using Your Calculator

1) Your calculator can make questions a lot easier for you but only if you <u>know how to use it</u>. Make sure you know what the different buttons do and how to use them.

2) Remember to check your calculator is in <u>degrees mode</u>. This is important for <u>trigonometry</u> questions.

3) If you're working out a <u>big calculation</u> on your calculator, it's best to do it in <u>stages</u> and use the <u>memory</u> to store the answers to the different parts.
   If you try and do it all in one go, it's too easy to mess it up.

4) If you're going to be a renegade and do a question all in one go on your calculator, use <u>brackets</u> so the calculator knows which bits to do first.

REMEMBER: Golden Rule number 2 <u>still applies</u>, even if you're using a calculator — you should still <u>write down all the steps</u> you are doing so the examiner can see the <u>method</u> you're using.

Answers

Section One — Numerical Skills

Page 3 — Fractions

Q1 a) $\dfrac{3}{8} \times 1\dfrac{5}{12} = \dfrac{3}{8} \times \dfrac{17}{12} = \dfrac{1}{8} \times \dfrac{17}{4}$

$= \dfrac{1 \times 17}{8 \times 4} = \dfrac{17}{32}$

[2 marks available — 1 mark for converting the mixed number to an improper fraction and showing a correct method for multiplying fractions, 1 mark for the correct answer in its simplest form]

b) $1\dfrac{7}{9} \div 2\dfrac{2}{3} = \dfrac{16}{9} \div \dfrac{8}{3} = \dfrac{16}{9} \times \dfrac{3}{8} = \dfrac{2}{3} \times \dfrac{1}{1} = \dfrac{2}{3}$

[2 marks available — 1 mark for converting the mixed numbers to improper fractions and showing a correct method for dividing fractions, 1 mark for the correct answer in its simplest form]

c) $4\dfrac{1}{9} + 2\dfrac{2}{27} = \dfrac{37}{9} + \dfrac{56}{27}$

$= \dfrac{111}{27} + \dfrac{56}{27} = \dfrac{111 + 56}{27}$

$= \dfrac{167}{27} = 6\dfrac{5}{27}$

[2 marks available — 1 mark for correctly finding a common denominator, 1 mark for the correct answer]

d) $9\dfrac{1}{4} - 5\dfrac{2}{3} = \dfrac{37}{4} - \dfrac{17}{3}$

$= \dfrac{111}{12} - \dfrac{68}{12} = \dfrac{111 - 68}{12}$

$= \dfrac{43}{12} = 3\dfrac{7}{12}$

[2 marks available — 1 mark for correctly finding a common denominator, 1 mark for the correct answer]

Q2 $\left(1\dfrac{1}{5} - \dfrac{2}{3}\right) \div \dfrac{3}{5} = \left(\dfrac{6}{5} - \dfrac{2}{3}\right) \div \dfrac{3}{5}$

$= \left(\dfrac{18}{15} - \dfrac{10}{15}\right) \div \dfrac{3}{5} = \dfrac{8}{15} \div \dfrac{3}{5}$

$= \dfrac{8}{15} \times \dfrac{5}{3} = \dfrac{8}{3} \times \dfrac{1}{3} = \dfrac{8}{9}$

[3 marks available — 1 mark for subtracting the fractions in brackets, 1 mark for showing a correct method for dividing fractions, 1 mark for the correct answer in its simplest form]

Page 5 — Percentages

Q1 After 3 months: £160 000 × 0.975 = £156 000
After the next 3 months: £156 000 × 0.98 = £152 880
So the price is £152 880 after 6 months.

[3 marks available — 1 mark for multiplying the initial value by 0.975, 1 mark for multiplying the new value by 0.98, 1 mark for the correct answer]

You'd get the marks if you worked out the % decrease and subtracted it each time.

Page 6 — Compound Growth and Decay

Q1 In the 4th year, Alasdair's rent will be:
£600 × 1.035⁴ = £688.5138... = £688.51 (2 d.p.)

[3 marks available — 1 mark for using the multiplier 1.035, 1 mark for raising the multiplier to the power 4, 1 mark for the correct answer]

Page 7 — Reverse Percentages

Q1 900 ml = 75%
12 ml = 1%
1200 ml = 100%
So the original amount of cordial in a bottle was 1200 ml.

[3 marks available — 1 mark for recognising that 900 ml is 75%, 1 mark for a correct method to find 100%, 1 mark for the correct answer]

Q2 1500 g = 142%
10.56338... g = 1%
1056.338... g = 100%
So the mass of the kitten one month ago was 1056 g to the nearest gram.

[3 marks available — 1 mark for recognising that 1500 g is 142%, 1 mark for a correct method to find 100%, 1 mark for the correct answer]

Page 8 — The Laws of Indices

Q1 a) $(g^6)^{\frac{1}{2}} \times g^2 = g^{6 \times \frac{1}{2}} \times g^2 = g^{3+2} = g^5$ *[1 mark]*

b) $2h^5j^{-2} \times 3h^2j^4 = (2 \times 3)h^{5+2}j^{-2+4} = 6h^7j^2$
[2 marks available — 2 marks for the correct answer, otherwise 1 mark for two of 6, h^7 and j^2 correct]

Q2 a) $625^{\frac{3}{4}} = \left(625^{\frac{1}{4}}\right)^3 = \left(\sqrt[4]{625}\right)^3 = 5^3 = 125$
[2 marks available — 1 mark for interpreting the index correctly, 1 mark for correct answer]
You might have to use some trial and error to find the root if you didn't know that $5^4 = 625$.

b) $25^{-\frac{1}{2}} = \dfrac{1}{25^{\frac{1}{2}}} = \dfrac{1}{\sqrt{25}} = \dfrac{1}{5}$
[2 marks available — 1 mark for interpreting the index correctly, 1 mark for correct answer]

c) $\left(\dfrac{27}{64}\right)^{-\frac{1}{3}} = \left(\dfrac{64}{27}\right)^{\frac{1}{3}} = \dfrac{\sqrt[3]{64}}{\sqrt[3]{27}} = \dfrac{4}{3}$
[2 marks available — 1 mark for interpreting the index correctly, 1 mark for correct answer]

Answers

Page 10 — Scientific Notation

Q1 60 kg = 60 000 g
So the catering company uses
$40 \times 60\ 000$ grains $= (4 \times 10^1) \times (6 \times 10^4)$
$= (4 \times 6) \times (10^1 \times 10^4)$
$= 24 \times 10^5$
$= 2.4 \times 10^6$ grains of rice.

*[2 marks available — 1 mark for a correct method,
1 mark for the correct answer in scientific notation]*

Page 11 — Manipulating Surds

Q1 $\sqrt{162} = \sqrt{81 \times 2} = 9\sqrt{2}$ *[1 mark]*
$\sqrt{72} = \sqrt{36 \times 2} = 6\sqrt{2}$ *[1 mark]*
So $\sqrt{162} - \sqrt{72} = 9\sqrt{2} - 6\sqrt{2} = 3\sqrt{2}$ *[1 mark]*

[3 marks available in total — as above]

Q2 $\dfrac{9}{\sqrt{18}} = \dfrac{9}{\sqrt{9 \times 2}} = \dfrac{9}{3\sqrt{2}} = \dfrac{3}{\sqrt{2}} = \dfrac{3\sqrt{2}}{2}$

*[3 marks available — 1 mark for simplifying the surd,
1 mark for rationalising the denominator, 1 mark for
the correct final answer in its simplest form]*

You could have done the first two steps the other way
round — i.e. rationalised the denominator then simplified
the surd.

Page 12 — Revision Questions

Q1 Divide top and bottom by the same number till they
won't go any further.

Q2 a) $74 \div 9 = 8$ remainder 2, so $\dfrac{74}{9} = 8\dfrac{2}{9}$

b) $4\dfrac{5}{7} = 4 + \dfrac{5}{7} = \dfrac{28}{7} + \dfrac{5}{7} = \dfrac{28 + 5}{7} = \dfrac{33}{7}$

Q3 a) $\dfrac{7}{9}$ of 270 kg $= (270 \div 9) \times 7 = 30 \times 7 = 210$ kg

b) $\dfrac{88}{56} = \dfrac{11}{7}$

Q4 Multiplying: Multiply top and bottom numbers
separately.
Dividing: Turn the second fraction upside down,
then multiply.
Adding/subtracting: Put fractions over a common
denominator, then add/subtract the numerators.

Q5 a) $\dfrac{2}{11} \times \dfrac{7}{9} = \dfrac{2 \times 7}{11 \times 9} = \dfrac{14}{99}$

b) $5\dfrac{1}{2} \div 1\dfrac{3}{4} = \dfrac{11}{2} \div \dfrac{7}{4}$
$= \dfrac{11}{2} \times \dfrac{4}{7} = 11 \times \dfrac{2}{7}$
$= \dfrac{22}{7}$ or $3\dfrac{1}{7}$

c) $\dfrac{5}{8} - \dfrac{1}{6} = \dfrac{15}{24} - \dfrac{4}{24} = \dfrac{15 - 4}{24} = \dfrac{11}{24}$

d) $3\dfrac{3}{10} + 4\dfrac{1}{4} = \dfrac{33}{10} + \dfrac{17}{4}$
$= \dfrac{66}{20} + \dfrac{85}{20}$
$= \dfrac{151}{20}$ or $7\dfrac{11}{20}$

Q6 $\dfrac{6}{5}\left(\dfrac{2}{3} - \dfrac{1}{8}\right) = \dfrac{6}{5}\left(\dfrac{16}{24} - \dfrac{3}{24}\right)$
$= \dfrac{6}{5} \times \dfrac{13}{24} = \dfrac{1}{5} \times \dfrac{13}{4}$
$= \dfrac{1 \times 13}{5 \times 4} = \dfrac{13}{20}$

Q7 a) The decider is 3, so leave the last digit as 6,
giving 427.96

b) The decider is 6, so round up to 428.0

c) The decider is 7, so round up to 430

d) The decider is 6, so round up to 428.0

Q8 The decider is 4, so leave the last digit as 8,
giving 0.00178

Q9 a) 20% of 95 $= 0.2 \times 95 = 19$

b) 95 as a percentage of 20:
$(95 \div 20) \times 100 = 475\%$

Q10 percentage change $= (\text{change} \div \text{original}) \times 100$

Q11 £800 − £520 = £280 decrease
$(280 \div 800) \times 100 = 35\%$ decrease

Q12 Multiplier $= 1 + 0.18 = 1.18$
New value $= £2520 \times 1.18 = £2973.60$

Q13 $N = N_0 \times (\text{multiplier})^n$

Q14 a) $N = 80(1.07)^{10} = £157.37$ (to the nearest penny)

b) Use trial and error:
If $n = 13$, $N = 80(1.07)^{13} = 192.7876$
If $n = 14$, $N = 80(1.07)^{14} = 206.282732$
So it will be 14 years before the card is worth over
£200.

Q15 20.24 m = 115%
0.176 m = 1%
17.6 m = 100%
So the original height was 17.6 metres.

Q16 260 = 65%
4 = 1%
400 = 100%
So there were 400 football stickers in his collection.

Q17 a) $x^3 \times x^6 = x^{3+6} = x^9$
b) $y^7 \div y^5 = y^{7-5} = y^2$
c) $(z^3)^4 = z^{3 \times 4} = z^{12}$

Q18 a) $225^{\frac{1}{2}} = \sqrt{225} = 15$
b) $36^{-\frac{1}{2}} = \dfrac{1}{\sqrt{36}} = \dfrac{1}{6}$
c) $8^{\frac{4}{3}} = (\sqrt[3]{8})^4 = 2^4 = 16$

Answers

Q19 $\dfrac{1}{\sqrt[4]{a}} = \dfrac{1}{a^{\frac{1}{4}}} = a^{-\frac{1}{4}}$

Q20 1. The front number must always be between 1 and 10.
2. The power of 10, n, is how far the decimal point moves.
3. n is positive for big numbers, and negative for small numbers.

Q21 a) To get from 970 000 to 9.7, the decimal point moves 5 places (and it's a big number), so $970\,000 = 9.7 \times 10^5$

b) To get from 3 560 000 000 to 3.56, the decimal point moves 9 places (and it's a big number), so $3\,560\,000\,000 = 3.56 \times 10^9$

c) To get from 0.00000275 to 2.75, the decimal point moves 6 places (and it's a small number), so $0.00000275 = 2.75 \times 10^{-6}$

Q22 The decimal point moves 3 places, and the power is negative, which means it's a small number, so $4.56 \times 10^{-3} = 0.00456$
The decimal point moves 5 places, and the power is positive, which means it's a big number, so $2.7 \times 10^5 = 270\,000$

Q23 a) $(3.2 \times 10^6) \div (1.6 \times 10^3) = (3.2 \div 1.6) \times (10^6 \div 10^3)$
$= 2 \times 10^{6-3} = 2 \times 10^3$

b) $(1.75 \times 10^{12}) + (9.89 \times 10^{11})$
$= (1.75 \times 10^{12}) + (0.989 \times 10^{12})$
$= (1.75 + 0.989) \times 10^{12} = 2.739 \times 10^{12}$

Q24 After 30 minutes:
$(3.1 \times 10^8) \times 2^3 = 24.8 \times 10^8 = 2.48 \times 10^9$

Q25 a) $\sqrt{27} = \sqrt{9 \times 3} = \sqrt{9} \times \sqrt{3} = 3\sqrt{3}$

b) $\dfrac{\sqrt{125}}{\sqrt{5}} = \sqrt{\dfrac{125}{5}} = \sqrt{25} = 5$

Q26 $\sqrt{98} + 3\sqrt{8} - \sqrt{200}$
$= \sqrt{49 \times 2} + 3\sqrt{4 \times 2} - \sqrt{100 \times 2}$
$= \sqrt{49}\sqrt{2} + 3\sqrt{4}\sqrt{2} - \sqrt{100}\sqrt{2}$
$= 7\sqrt{2} + 6\sqrt{2} - 10\sqrt{2} = 3\sqrt{2}$

Q27 a) $\dfrac{2}{\sqrt{7}} = \dfrac{2\sqrt{7}}{\sqrt{7}\sqrt{7}} = \dfrac{2\sqrt{7}}{7}$

b) $\dfrac{4}{\sqrt{12}} = \dfrac{4}{\sqrt{4 \times 3}} = \dfrac{4}{2\sqrt{3}} = \dfrac{2}{\sqrt{3}} = \dfrac{2\sqrt{3}}{3}$

Section Two — Algebraic Skills

Page 13 — Expanding Brackets

Q1 a) $(y + 4)(y - 5) = (y \times y) + (y \times -5) + (4 \times y) + (4 \times -5)$
$= y^2 - 5y + 4y - 20$
$= y^2 - y - 20$

[2 marks available — 1 mark for starting to multiply out brackets, 1 mark for correct answer with like terms collected]

b) $(2p - 3)^2 = (2p - 3)(2p - 3)$
$= 4p^2 - 6p - 6p + 9$
$= 4p^2 - 12p + 9$

[2 marks available — 1 mark for starting to multiply out brackets, 1 mark for correct answer with like terms collected]

Q2 a) $(x - 2)(4x^2 - x + 2) = x(4x^2 - x + 2) - 2(4x^2 - x + 2)$
$= 4x^3 - x^2 + 2x - 8x^2 + 2x - 4$
$= 4x^3 - 9x^2 + 4x - 4$

[3 marks available — 1 mark for starting to multiply out brackets, 1 mark for completely multiplying out brackets, 1 mark for simplified answer with like terms collected]

b) $(x^2 - x + 9)(x + 1) = (x + 1)(x^2 - x + 9)$
$= x(x^2 - x + 9) + 1(x^2 - x + 9)$
$= x^3 - x^2 + 9x + x^2 - x + 9$
$= x^3 + 8x + 9$

[3 marks available — 1 mark for starting to multiply out brackets, 1 mark for completely multiplying out brackets, 1 mark for simplified answer with like terms collected]

Page 14 — Expanding Brackets

Q1 a) $2(x - 1) + 9(3x + 2) = 2x - 2 + 27x + 18$
$= 29x + 16$

[2 marks available — 1 mark for multiplying out both brackets, 1 mark for correct answer with like terms collected]

b) $2(p + q) - 3(p - 1)^2 = 2(p + q) - 3(p - 1)(p - 1)$
$= 2p + 2q - 3(p^2 - 2p + 1)$
$= 2p + 2q - 3p^2 + 6p - 3$
$= 2q - 3p^2 + 8p - 3$

[3 marks available — 1 mark for starting to multiply out squared bracket, 1 mark for multiplying out all brackets, 1 mark for correct answer with like terms collected]

Answers

Q2 Area of triangle $= \frac{1}{2} \times$ base $\times$ height

$$= \frac{1}{2}(2x + 4)(x^2 + 3x + 4)$$
$$= (x + 2)(x^2 + 3x + 4)$$
$$= x(x^2 + 3x + 4) + 2(x^2 + 3x + 4)$$
$$= x^3 + 3x^2 + 4x + 2x^2 + 6x + 8$$
$$= x^3 + 5x^2 + 10x + 8 \text{ cm}^2$$

[3 marks available — 1 mark for substituting the measurements into the formula for the area of a triangle, 1 mark for multiplying out brackets, 1 mark for the correct answer with like terms collected]

Page 15 — Factorising

Q1 $3y(2x + 5y)$ *[1 mark]*

Remember, it's easy to check that you've factorised correctly — just multiply out the brackets and make sure you get back to the original expression.

Q2 $x^2 - 16y^2 = (x + 4y)(x - 4y)$ *[1 mark]*

Q3 $20x^2 - 45y^2 = 5(4x^2 - 9y^2) = 5(2x + 3y)(2x - 3y)$

[2 marks available — 1 mark for taking out a factor of 5, 1 mark for correct answer]

Q4 $\dfrac{6x - 42}{x^2 - 49} = \dfrac{6(x - 7)}{(x + 7)(x - 7)} = \dfrac{6}{x + 7}$

[3 marks available — 1 mark for factorising numerator, 1 mark for factorising denominator, 1 mark for correct answer]

Page 16 — Solving Equations

Q1 $2x + 5 = 17 - 4x$
$2x = 12 - 4x$
$6x = 12$
$x = 2$

[2 marks available — 1 mark for rearranging equation to 6x = 12, 1 mark for correct answer]

Q2 $4(y + 3) = 3y + 16$
$4y + 12 = 3y + 16$
$y = 4$

[2 marks available — 1 mark for multiplying out brackets, 1 mark for correct answer]

Q3 $\dfrac{3x + 2}{5} = \dfrac{5x + 6}{9}$
$9(3x + 2) = 5(5x + 6)$
$27x + 18 = 25x + 30$
$2x = 12$
$x = 6$

[3 marks available — 1 mark for getting rid of fractions, 1 mark for multiplying out brackets, 1 mark for correct answer]

Page 17 — Solving Equations

Q1 $\dfrac{2}{x} + 8 = \dfrac{82}{x}$
$2 + 8x = 82$
$8x = 80$
$x = 10$

[3 marks available — 1 mark for getting rid of fractions, 1 mark for rearranging to 8x = 80, 1 mark for correct answer]

Q2 $\dfrac{3x - 2}{2} - \dfrac{4x - 5}{3} = 2$
$3(3x - 2) - 2(4x - 5) = 12$
$9x - 6 - 8x + 10 = 12$
$x = 8$

[3 marks available — 1 mark for getting rid of fractions, 1 mark for multiplying out brackets, 1 mark for correct answer]

Page 18 — Inequalities

Q1 a) $11x + 3 < 42 - 2x$
$11x < 39 - 2x$
$13x < 39$
$x < 3$

[2 marks available — 1 mark for rearranging the inequality to 13x < 39, 1 mark for correct answer]

b) $6 - 4x \geq 18$
$-4x \geq 12$
$x \leq -3$

[2 marks available — 1 mark for rearranging the inequality to -4x ≥ 12, 1 mark for correct answer]

Q2 $20 > 3x - 2(x + 2)$
$20 > 3x - 2x - 4$
$20 > x - 4$
$24 > x$

[3 marks available — 1 mark for expanding bracket, 1 mark for collecting like terms, 1 mark for correct answer]

Page 19 — Rearranging Formulas

Q1 $p = \dfrac{q}{7} + 2r$
$7p = q + 14r$
$q = 7(p - 2r)$ or $7p - 14r$

[2 marks available — 1 mark for getting rid of fraction, 1 mark for correct answer]

Q2 $b = \dfrac{703w}{h^2}$
$b \times h^2 = 703w$
$w = \dfrac{b \times h^2}{703}$

[2 marks available — 1 mark for getting rid of fraction, 1 mark for correct answer]

Answers

Page 20 — Rearranging Formulas

Q1 a) $x = \dfrac{y^2}{4}$

$4x = y^2$

$y = \pm 2\sqrt{x}$

[2 marks available — 2 marks for fully correct answer, otherwise 1 mark for partially correct answer, e.g. $2\sqrt{x}$ or $\pm\sqrt{4x}$]

Remember the ± when you take a square root.

b) $x = \dfrac{y}{y - z}$

$x(y - z) = y$

$xy - xz = y$

$xy - y = xz$

$y(x - 1) = xz$

$y = \dfrac{xz}{x - 1}$

[3 marks available — 1 mark for getting rid of fraction, 1 mark for rearranging equation and factorising, 1 mark for correct answer]

Q2 $b = \dfrac{703w}{h^2}$

$b \times h^2 = 703w$

$h^2 = \dfrac{703w}{b}$

$h = \sqrt{\dfrac{703w}{b}}$

[3 marks available — 1 mark for getting rid of fraction, 1 mark for rearranging equation, 1 mark for correct answer]

Height (h) has to be positive so you can ignore the negative square root.

Page 21 — Functions and Straight Line Graphs

Q1 a) $f(9) = \dfrac{9^2}{\sqrt{9} - 2} = \dfrac{81}{3 - 2} = 81$

[2 marks available — 1 mark for correct substitution, 1 mark for correct answer]

Q2

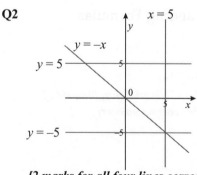

[2 marks for all four lines correct, otherwise 1 mark for two or three lines correct]

Page 23 — Straight Line Graphs

Q1 Change in $y = 30 - (-10) = 40$

Change in $x = -5 - 3 = -8$

Gradient $= \dfrac{\text{change in } y}{\text{change in } x} = \dfrac{40}{-8} = -5$ *[1 mark]*

Q2 a) $7x - 3y + 10 = 0 \Rightarrow 3y = 7x + 10$

$\Rightarrow y = \dfrac{7}{3}x + \dfrac{10}{3}$

So the gradient is $\dfrac{7}{3}$

[2 marks available — 1 mark for rearranging equation, 1 mark for identifying gradient]

b) $\left(0, \dfrac{10}{3}\right)$ *[1 mark]*

Q3 a) Gradient $= \dfrac{16 - 1}{9 - 0} = \dfrac{15}{9} = \dfrac{5}{3}$

$y - 1 = \dfrac{5}{3}(x - 0) \Rightarrow 3y - 3 = 5x$

$\Rightarrow 5x - 3y + 3 = 0$

[3 marks available — 1 mark for correct gradient, 1 mark for using a correct method to find the equation of a line, 1 mark for correct equation in the form ax + by + c = 0]

b) Gradient $= \dfrac{3 - (-1)}{21 - 9} = \dfrac{4}{12} = \dfrac{1}{3}$

$y - (-1) = \dfrac{1}{3}(x - 9) \Rightarrow y + 1 = \dfrac{1}{3}x - 3$

$\Rightarrow y = \dfrac{1}{3}x - 4$

[3 marks available — 1 mark for correct gradient, 1 mark for using a correct method to find the equation of a line, 1 mark for correct equation in the form y = mx + c]

Q4 $y - 5 = -2(x - 2) \Rightarrow y - 5 = -2x + 4$

$\Rightarrow 2x + y - 9 = 0$

[2 marks available — 1 mark for using a correct method to find the equation of a line, 1 mark for correct equation in the form ax + by + c = 0]

Page 24 — Factorising Quadratics

Q1 $(x + 5)(x - 3)$ *[1 mark]*

Always check your factorisation by multiplying out the brackets.

Q2 $x^2 - 9x + 20 = 0$

$(x - 4)(x - 5) = 0$

$x = 4$ or $x = 5$

[2 marks available — 1 mark for correct factorisation, 1 mark for correct solutions to the equation]

Answers

Page 25 — Factorising Quadratics

Q1 $(2x + 3)(x - 4)$

[2 marks available — 1 mark for $(2x \pm 3)(x \pm 4)$, 1 mark for correct answer]

Q2 $3x^2 + 10x - 8 = 0$
$(3x - 2)(x + 4) = 0$
$x = \dfrac{2}{3}$ or $x = -4$

[3 marks available — 1 mark for $(3x \pm 2)(x \pm 4)$, 1 mark for both factors correct, 1 mark for correct solutions to equation]

Q3 $(3x + 2)(x + 10)$

[2 marks available — 1 mark for $(3x \pm 2)(x \pm 10)$, 1 mark for correct answer]

Q4 $5x^2 - 13x = 6$
$5x^2 - 13x - 6 = 0$
$(5x + 2)(x - 3) = 0$
$x = -\dfrac{2}{5}$ or $x = 3$

[3 marks available — 1 mark for $(5x \pm 2)(x \pm 3)$, 1 mark for both factors correct, 1 mark for correct solutions to equation]

Page 26 — The Quadratic Formula

Q1 $x^2 + 10x - 4 = 0 \Rightarrow a = 1, b = 10, c = -4$

$$x = \frac{-10 \pm \sqrt{10^2 - (4 \times 1 \times -4)}}{2 \times 1}$$
$$= \frac{-10 \pm \sqrt{116}}{2}$$
$x = 0.39$ or -10.39 (2 d.p.)

[3 marks available — 1 mark for correct substitution into quadratic formula, 1 mark for evaluating discriminant, 1 mark for both correct solutions]

Q2 $2x + \dfrac{3}{x - 2} = -2$
$2x(x - 2) + 3 = -2(x - 2)$
$2x^2 - 4x + 3 = -2x + 4$
$2x^2 - 2x - 1 = 0$
Use quadratic formula: $a = 2, b = -2, c = -1$

$$x = \frac{-(-2) \pm \sqrt{(-2)^2 - (4 \times 2 \times -1)}}{2 \times 2}$$
$$= \frac{2 \pm \sqrt{12}}{4}$$
$$= \frac{2 \pm 2\sqrt{3}}{4} = \frac{1 \pm \sqrt{3}}{2}$$

[4 marks available — 1 mark for multiplying by $(x - 2)$ and rearranging into standard quadratic form, 1 mark for correct substitution into quadratic formula, 1 mark for evaluating discriminant, 1 mark for both correct solutions as simplified surds]

Page 27 — Completing the Square

Q1 $(x - 6)^2 = x^2 - 12x + 36$
$(x - 6)^2 - 13 = x^2 - 12x + 36 - 13 = x^2 - 12x + 23$
So $x^2 - 12x + 23 = (x - 6)^2 - 13$

[2 marks available — 1 mark for correct bracket with square, 1 mark for fully correct answer]

Q2 $x^2 + 10x + 7 = 0$
$(x + 5)^2 - 25 + 7 = 0$
$(x + 5)^2 - 18 = 0$
$(x + 5)^2 = 18$
$(x + 5) = \pm\sqrt{18}$
$x = -5 \pm \sqrt{18}$
$x = -5 \pm 3\sqrt{2}$

[4 marks available — 1 mark for writing $(x + 5)^2$, 1 mark for completing the square correctly, 1 mark for solving to find x, 1 mark for both correct solutions as simplified surds]

Remember the ± when you take the square root.

Page 28 — Quadratic Graphs

Q1 a) $p = -5$ *[1 mark]*

b) $5 = k(6 - 5)^2 - 2$
$7 = k(1)^2$
$k = 7$

[2 marks available — 1 mark for substituting (6, 5) into the equation, 1 mark for correct value of k]

Page 29 — Sketching Quadratics

Q1 $(x - 2)(x + 3)$

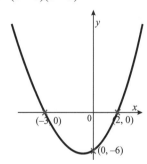

[3 marks available — 1 mark for factorising to find correct x-intercepts, 1 mark for correct y-intercept, 1 mark for correct shape]

Answers

Q2

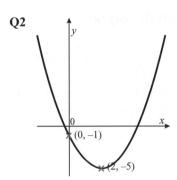

[3 marks available — 1 mark for correct coordinates of turning point, 1 mark for correct shape and position of graph, 1 mark for correct y-intercept]

Page 30 — The Discriminant

Q1 a) $a = 4$, $b = 28$, $c = 49$
$b^2 - 4ac = 28^2 - 4 \times 4 \times 49 = 784 - 784 = 0$
So there is one real, repeated root.
[2 marks available — 1 mark for correct discriminant, 1 mark for correct conclusion]

b) $a = 3$, $b = 3$, $c = 1$
$b^2 - 4ac = 3^2 - 4 \times 3 \times 1 = 9 - 12 = -3$
$-3 < 0$ so there are no real roots.
[2 marks available — 1 mark for correct discriminant, 1 mark for correct conclusion]

c) $a = 2$, $b = 9$, $c = -5$
$b^2 - 4ac = 9^2 - 4 \times 2 \times (-5) = 81 + 40 = 121$
$121 > 0$ so there are two real, distinct roots.
[2 marks available — 1 mark for correct discriminant, 1 mark for correct conclusion]

Page 31 — Algebraic Fractions

Q1 $\dfrac{x^4 - 4y^2}{x^3 - 2xy} = \dfrac{(x^2 - 2y)(x^2 + 2y)}{x(x^2 - 2y)} = \dfrac{x^2 + 2y}{x}$

[3 mark available — 1 mark for factorising numerator, 1 mark for factorising denominator, 1 mark for correct answer]

Q2 $\dfrac{y^2}{9(x - 2)} \div \dfrac{y}{6x - 12} = \dfrac{y^2}{9(x - 2)} \times \dfrac{6x - 12}{y}$
$= \dfrac{y^{\cancel{2}}}{^3\cancel{9}(x - \cancel{2})} \times \dfrac{^2\cancel{6}(x - \cancel{2})}{\cancel{y}} = \dfrac{2y}{3}$

[3 marks available — 1 mark for turning the second fraction upside down and multiplying, 1 mark for cancelling any term, 1 mark for fully simplified answer]

Q3 $\dfrac{2}{x + 5} + \dfrac{3}{x - 2} = \dfrac{2(x - 2) + 3(x + 5)}{(x - 2)(x + 5)}$
$= \dfrac{2x - 4 + 3x + 15}{(x - 2)(x + 5)}$
$= \dfrac{5x + 11}{(x - 2)(x + 5)}$

[3 marks available — 1 mark for putting over common denominator, 1 mark for multiplying out brackets in numerator, 1 mark for correct answer]

Page 32 — Simultaneous Equations

Q1 $2x - 10 = 4y \implies 2x - 4y = 10$ (1)
$3y = 5x - 18 \implies 5x - 3y = 18$ (2)
$(1) \times 5$: $10x - 20y = 50$ (3)
$(2) \times 2$: $10x - 6y = 36$ (4)
$(3) - (4)$: $-14y = 14$
              $y = -1$
Sub into (1): $2x - 4 \times (-1) = 10$
                  $2x = 6$
                   $x = 3$
Solution: $x = 3$, $y = -1$
[3 marks available — 1 mark for attempting to scale equations to produce (3) and (4), 1 mark for a valid strategy that leads to two solutions, 1 mark for correct values of x and y]

An equally correct method would be to first eliminate y in order to find x and then to substitute the value of x back into one of the equations to find y.

Q2 $10x + 9y = 35$ (1)
$6x - 3y = 7$ (2)
$(2) \times 3$: $18x - 9y = 21$ (3)
$(1) + (3)$: $28x = 56$
             $x = 2$
Sub into (2): $6 \times 2 - 3y = 7$
                $-3y = -5$
                  $y = \dfrac{5}{3}$
Solution : $x = 2$, $y = \dfrac{5}{3}$
[3 marks available — 1 mark for attempting to scale equations to produce (3), 1 mark for a valid strategy that leads to two solutions, 1 mark for correct values of x and y]

Answers

Page 33 — Simultaneous Equations

Q1 a) $y = 2x - 3 \Rightarrow y - 2x = -3$ (1)

$y = 6 - x \Rightarrow y + x = 6$ (2)

(2) − (1): $3x = 9$

$x = 3$

Sub into (2): $y + 3 = 6 \Rightarrow y = 3$

Solution: $x = 3$, $y = 3$ so the lines intersect at (3, 3)

[2 marks available — 1 mark for a valid strategy that leads to two solutions, 1 mark for correct values of x and y]

b) $x + 5y = 25$ (1)

$y = 2x + 5 \Rightarrow 2x - y = -5$ (2)

(1) × 2: $2x + 10y = 50$ (3)

(3) − (2): $11y = 55$

$y = 5$

Sub into (2): $2x - 5 = -5$

$2x = 0$

$x = 0$

Solution: $x = 0$, $y = 5$ so the lines intersect at (0, 5)

[3 marks available — 1 mark for attempting to scale equations to produce (3), 1 mark for a valid strategy that leads to two solutions, 1 mark for correct values of x and y]

Page 34 — Revision Questions

Q1 a) $3(2x + 1) = (3 \times 2x) + (3 \times 1) = 6x + 3$

b) $(x + 2)(x - 3) = x^2 - 3x + 2x - 6 = x^2 - x - 6$

c) $(x + 3)(x + 5) = x^2 + 5x + 3x + 15 = x^2 + 8x + 15$

Q2 a) $(7x - 1)(2x^2 + 10x - 1)$

$= 14x^3 + 70x^2 - 7x - 2x^2 - 10x + 1$

$= 14x^3 + 68x^2 - 17x + 1$

b) $5(5x + 7) + 2(7x + 2) = 25x + 35 + 14x + 4$

$= 39x + 39$

Q3 a) $8x - 2xy^2 = 2x(4 - y^2) = 2x(2 + y)(2 - y)$

b) $(7 + 9pq)(7 - 9pq)$

c) $12x^2 - 48y^2 = 12(x^2 - 4y^2) = 12(x + 2y)(x - 2y)$

Q4 a) $5(x + 2) = 8 + 4(5 - x)$

$5x + 10 = 8 + 20 - 4x$

$9x = 18$

$x = 2$

b) $\dfrac{9x - 2}{2} = \dfrac{3x + 1}{9}$

$9(9x - 2) = 2(3x + 1)$

$81x - 18 = 6x + 2$

$75x = 20$

$x = \dfrac{4}{15}$

Q5 a) $4x + 3 \le 6x + 7$

$-2x \le 4$

$x \ge -2$

Remember to flip the inequality sign when you divide by a negative number.

b) $\dfrac{x}{5} + 9 > -20$

$x + 45 > -100$

$x > -145$

Q6 a) $\dfrac{p}{p + y} = 4$

$p = 4(p + y)$

$p = 4p + 4y$

$3p = -4y$

$p = -\dfrac{4y}{3}$

b) $\dfrac{1}{p} = \dfrac{1}{q} + \dfrac{1}{r}$

$qr = pr + pq$

$qr = p(r + q)$

$p = \dfrac{qr}{r + q}$

Q7 a) $5x + 2y = 1 \Rightarrow y = -\dfrac{5}{2}x + \dfrac{1}{2}$

Gradient $= -\dfrac{5}{2}$, y-intercept $= \dfrac{1}{2}$

b) $-y + 1 = 3x - 9 \Rightarrow y = -3x + 10$

Gradient $= -3$, y-intercept $= 10$

c) $3x = 2y \Rightarrow y = \dfrac{3}{2}x$

Gradient $= \dfrac{3}{2}$, y-intercept $= 0$

Q8 Gradient $= \dfrac{-3 - (-6)}{6 - 3} = \dfrac{3}{3} = 1$

$y - (-6) = 1(x - 3) \Rightarrow y = x - 9$

Q9 $y - 9 = -3(x - 1) \Rightarrow y = -3x + 12$

Q10 a) $x^2 + 9x + 18 = 0$

$(x + 3)(x + 6) = 0$

$x = -3$ or $x = -6$

b) $5x^2 - 17x - 12 = 0$

$(5x + 3)(x - 4) = 0$

$5x = -3$ or $x = 4$

$x = -\dfrac{3}{5}$ or $x = 4$

Q11 a) $x^2 + x - 4 = 0$

$a = 1$, $b = 1$, $c = -4$

$x = \dfrac{-1 \pm \sqrt{1^2 - (4 \times 1 \times (-4))}}{2 \times 1}$

$= \dfrac{-1 \pm \sqrt{17}}{2}$

$x = 1.56$ or $x = -2.56$ (2 d.p.)

b) $5x^2 + 6x - 2 = 0$

$a = 5$, $b = 6$, $c = -2$

$x = \dfrac{-6 \pm \sqrt{6^2 - (4 \times 5 \times -2)}}{2 \times 5}$

$= \dfrac{-6 \pm \sqrt{76}}{10}$

$x = 0.27$ or $x = -1.47$ (2 d.p.)

Answers

c)
$$(2x + 3)^2 = 15$$
$$4x^2 + 12x + 9 = 15$$
$$4x^2 + 12x - 6 = 0$$
$$2x^2 + 6x - 3 = 0$$
$$a = 2, b = 6, c = -3$$
$$x = \frac{-6 \pm \sqrt{6^2 - 4 \times 2 \times (-3)}}{2 \times 2}$$
$$= \frac{-6 \pm \sqrt{60}}{4}$$
$$x = 0.44 \text{ or } x = -3.44 \text{ (2 d.p.)}$$

Q12 a)
$$x^2 + 12x + 15 = 0$$
$$(x + 6)^2 - 36 + 15 = 0$$
$$(x + 6)^2 - 21 = 0$$
$$x = -6 \pm \sqrt{21}$$

b)
$$x^2 - 6x - 2 = 0$$
$$(x - 3)^2 - 9 - 2 = 0$$
$$(x - 3)^2 - 11 = 0$$
$$x = 3 \pm \sqrt{11}$$

Q13 Substitute (5, 10) into the equation:
$$10 = k(5)^2$$
$$10 = 25k$$
$$k = \frac{2}{5}$$

Q14 If the graph has a turning point at (2, 5), then the completed square form of the equation is
$$y = (x - 2)^2 + 5.$$

Q15 a)

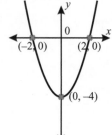

b)

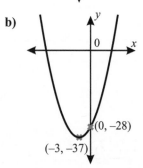

Q16 a) One real, repeated root

b) Two real, distinct roots

c) No real roots

Q17 a) $\dfrac{25xyz}{10x^2z^3} = \dfrac{5y}{2xz^2}$

b) $\dfrac{4x^2 - y^2}{(2x - y)^2} = \dfrac{(2x - y)(2x + y)}{(2x - y)^2} = \dfrac{2x + y}{2x - y}$

c) $\dfrac{3x}{x - y} \times \dfrac{4y}{(x - y)^2} = \dfrac{3x \times 4y}{(x - y)(x - y)^2} = \dfrac{12xy}{(x - y)^3}$

d) $\dfrac{12x}{x + 2} \div \dfrac{3}{x^2 + 4x + 4} = \dfrac{12x}{x + 2} \times \dfrac{x^2 + 4x + 4}{3}$
$$= \dfrac{4x}{x + 2} \times \dfrac{(x + 2)^2}{1}$$
$$= \dfrac{4x(x + 2)^2}{(x + 2)}$$
$$= 4x(x + 2)$$

Q18 $\dfrac{2}{x + 3} + \dfrac{1}{x - 1} = \dfrac{2(x - 1) + (x + 3)}{(x + 3)(x - 1)}$
$$= \dfrac{2x - 2 + x + 3}{(x + 3)(x - 1)}$$
$$= \dfrac{3x + 1}{(x + 3)(x - 1)}$$

Q19
$$5y + 4x = 23 \qquad (1)$$
$$3y - x = 7 \qquad (2)$$
$$(2) \times 4: \quad 12y - 4x = 28 \qquad (3)$$
$$(1) + (3): \quad 17y = 51$$
$$y = 3$$
Sub into (1): $\quad 4x + 5 \times 3 = 23$
$$4x = 8$$
$$x = 2$$
Solution: $x = 2, y = 3$

Q20
$$4y - 2x = 32 \qquad (1)$$
$$2y - 12 = 3x \Rightarrow 2y - 3x = 12 \quad (2)$$
$$(2) \times 2: \quad 4y - 6x = 24 \qquad (3)$$
$$(1) - (3): \quad 4x = 8$$
$$x = 2$$
Sub into (2): $\quad 2y - 3 \times 2 = 12$
$$2y - 6 = 12$$
$$2y = 18$$
$$y = 9$$
So the lines intersect at (2, 9).

Q21 Let t = cost of one cup of tea
and c = cost of one slice of cake
a) $2t + 3c = 9$ (1)

b) $4t + c = 8$ (2)

c) $(1) \times 2: \ 4t + 6c = 18 \qquad (3)$
$$(3) - (2): \ 5c = 10$$
$$c = 2$$
Sub into (1): $2t + 3 \times 2 = 9$
$$2t = 3$$
$$t = 1.5$$
So a cup of tea costs £1.50 and a slice of cake costs £2.

Answers

Section Three — Geometric Skills

Page 35 — Geometry

Q1 Since the triangle is isosceles, the angle next to x is $180° - 67° - 67° = 46°$ *[1 mark]*.
So the size of the angle x is $180° - 46° = 134°$ *[1 mark]*.
[2 marks available in total — as above]

Page 36 — Geometry

Q1 ABC and DBE are vertically opposite so DBE = 108°.
BDF and BEF are the interior angles of a regular
pentagon so BDF = BEF = $180° - \dfrac{360°}{5} = 108°$.
BEFD is a quadrilateral, and angles in a quadrilateral
add up to 360° so DFE = $360° - 108° - 108° - 108°$
$= 36°$.

*[3 marks available — 1 mark for correct size of DBE,
1 mark for correct size of BDF or BEF, 1 mark for
correct answer]*

Page 37 — Geometry Problems

Q1 One method is:
Find angle a (see diagram below) using allied angles:
$a = 180° - 145° = 35°$
Using vertically opposite angles: $b = a = 35°$
Using sum of angles in a triangle:
$c = 180° - (22° + 35°) = 123°$
And finally, using vertically opposite angles:
$x = c = 123°$

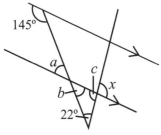

*[3 marks available — 1 mark for correct size of a,
1 mark for correct value of b, 1 mark for correct
answer]*

There are other ways you could have found x.
You'd still get all the marks so long as you show
all your working and make it clear which angles
you're finding as you go along.

Page 39 — Circle Geometry

Q1 Since $A\widehat{B}D$ and $A\widehat{C}D$ are angles in the same segment,
$A\widehat{B}D = A\widehat{C}D = 63°$ *[1 mark]*

Q2 $N\widehat{O}S$ is vertically opposite $Q\widehat{O}R$ so $N\widehat{O}S = 48°$.
The triangle NOS is right-angled since RT is a
perpendicular bisector.
So $P\widehat{S}Q = 180° - 90° - 48° = 42°$.
$Q\widehat{P}S = 90°$ since it is an angle in a semi-circle which
means the triangle QPS is right-angled.
So $P\widehat{Q}S = 180° - 90° - P\widehat{S}Q = 180° - 90° - 42° = 48°$.
*[3 marks available — 1 mark for correct size of
$N\widehat{O}S$, 1 mark for correct size of $P\widehat{S}Q$ with working,
1 mark for correct size of $P\widehat{Q}S$ with working]*

Page 40 — Similarity

Q1 Triangles ABC and ADE are similar.
Scale factor = $18 \div 12 = 1.5$
AD = $20 \times 1.5 = 30$ cm
BD = AD – AB = $30 - 20 = 10$ cm
*[2 marks available — 1 mark for correct scale factor,
1 mark for correct answer]*

You have to pick out the corresponding sides first.
Do this by matching the angles up.

Page 41 — Arcs and Sectors

Q1 a) Area of sector = $\dfrac{112}{360} \times \pi \times 4^2 = 15.64$ cm² (2 d.p.)

*[3 marks available — 1 mark for correct fraction,
1 mark for correct substitution into formula,
1 mark for correct answer]*

b) Arc length = $\dfrac{112}{360} \times \pi \times 2 \times 4 = 7.82$ cm (2 d.p.)

*[3 marks available — 1 mark for correct fraction,
1 mark for correct substitution into formula,
1 mark for correct answer]*

Page 42 — Volume

Q1 Volume of a sphere = $\dfrac{4}{3}\pi r^3 = \dfrac{4}{3} \times \pi \times 6^3 = 288\pi$ mm³
Volume of base = $250 \times 100 \times 20 = 500\ 000$ mm³
Volume of a post = $\pi \times 2.5^2 \times 200 = 1250\pi$ mm³
Total volume = $(5 \times 288\pi) + 500\ 000 + (6 \times 1250\pi)$
$= 528\ 085.83...$ mm³
$= 528\ 000$ mm³ (3 s.f.)

*[5 marks available — 1 mark for correct volume
of a sphere, 1 mark for correct volume of the base,
1 mark for correct volume of a post, 1 mark for
correct sum for total volume, 1 mark for correct final
answer to 3 s.f.]*

It's always best to keep your calculations exact
(i.e. in terms of π) right until the end.

Answers

Page 43 — Volume

Q1 Volume of sphere $= \frac{4}{3}\pi r^3 = \frac{4}{3}\pi \times 9^3 = 972\pi$

Volume of cone $= \frac{1}{3}\pi r^2 \times h = \frac{1}{3} \times \pi \times 9^2 \times h = 27\pi h$

$972\pi = 27\pi h \implies h = 36$ cm

[3 marks available — 1 mark for correct volume of the sphere, 1 mark for correct volume of the cone, 1 mark for correct value of h]

Q2 Volume of pyramid $= \frac{1}{3} \times$ base area $\times$ height

$= \frac{1}{3} \times 60^2 \times 110 = 132\,000$ cm

Volume of cone $= \frac{1}{3}\pi r^2 h = \frac{1}{3} \times \pi \times 34^2 \times 110$

$\qquad\qquad = 133\,161.64...$ cm

So the water does not overflow the cone since the volume of the cone is greater than the volume of the pyramid.

[3 marks available — 1 mark for correct volume of the pyramid, 1 mark for correct volume of the cone, 1 mark for correct conclusion]

Page 44 — Using Similarity

Q1 Scale factor for the smallest doll $= \frac{5}{10} = \frac{1}{2}$

Volume of the smallest doll $= 216 \times \left(\frac{1}{2}\right)^3 = 27$ cm³

Scale factor for the largest doll $= \frac{15}{10} = \frac{3}{2}$

Volume of the largest doll $= 216 \times \left(\frac{3}{2}\right)^3 = 729$ cm³

[3 marks available — 1 mark for either scale factor correct, 1 mark for correct volume of one of the dolls, 1 mark for correct volume of the other doll]

Interesting fact: the world-record breaking set of Russian dolls contains 51 dolls. The smallest doll is just over 3 mm tall.

Page 45 — Pythagoras' Theorem

Q1 $5^2 + 9^2 = AC^2$

$AC = \sqrt{25 + 81} = \sqrt{106}$

$AC = 10.3$ m (3 s.f.)

[2 marks available — 1 mark for correct use of formula, 1 mark for correct answer]

Q2

Length of horizontal side $= 10 - 6 = 4$

Length of vertical side $= 15 - 12 = 3$

$AB^2 = 4^2 + 3^2$

$AB = \sqrt{16 + 9} = \sqrt{25}$

$AB = 5$

[3 marks available — 1 mark for correctly determining lengths of the vertical and horizontal sides of the triangle, 1 mark for correct use of formula, 1 mark for correct answer]

Q3 $a^2 + b^2 = (2\sqrt{10})^2$

$a^2 + b^2 = 40$

Now find two square numbers that add up to 40:

$4 + 36 = 40$

$2^2 + 6^2 = 40$

Possible lengths are 2 cm and 6 cm.

[3 marks available — 1 mark for squaring $2\sqrt{10}$, 1 mark for finding two square numbers that add up to 40, 1 mark for a correct pair of possible side lengths]

Page 46 — Pythagoras' Theorem

Q1 a) $AH^2 = GH^2 + DG^2 + AD^2$

$\qquad = 12^2 + 5^2 + 7^2$ *[1 mark]*

$\qquad = \sqrt{144 + 25 + 49} = \sqrt{218}$ *[1 mark]*

$\qquad = 14.8$ cm (3 s.f.) *[1 mark]*

[3 marks available in total — as above]

b) $BP = \sqrt{BF^2 + FP^2} = \sqrt{5^2 + 3.5^2} = \sqrt{37.25}$

$CP = BP = \sqrt{37.25}$ (as BCHF is a rectangle and P is the midpoint of FH).

$P\widehat{B}C$ and $P\widehat{C}B$ are less than 90° so the only possible right-angle is $B\widehat{P}C$.

If the triangle is right-angled, then Pythagoras' theorem means $BP^2 + CP^2 = BC^2$:

$BP^2 + CP^2 = \left(\sqrt{37.25}\right)^2 + \left(\sqrt{37.25}\right)^2 = 74.5$

but $BC^2 = 7^2 = 49$ cm and $74.5 \neq 49$.

So the triangle is not right-angled.

[3 marks available — 1 mark for using Pythagoras to find BP or CP, 1 mark for evaluating $BP^2 + CP^2$ and BC^2, 1 mark for correct conclusion with fully correct working]

Answers

Page 47 — 3D Coordinates

Q1 D has x- and z-coordinates of 0 and the same
y-coordinate as B. So it has coordinates $(0, 4, 0)$.
E has the same x- and z-coordinates as C.
The y-distance between C and A is $4 - 3 = 1$
so the cube has side lengths of 1.
Therefore, the y-coordinate of E is 1.
So the coordinates are $(4, 1, 5)$.
*[2 marks available — 1 mark for correct coordinates
of D, 1 mark for correct coordinates of E]*

Page 48 — Vectors

Q1 $\overrightarrow{AB} = \overrightarrow{AC} + \overrightarrow{CB} = \mathbf{p} - 2\mathbf{q}$
$\overrightarrow{NA} = -\frac{1}{2}\overrightarrow{AB} = \mathbf{q} - \frac{1}{2}\mathbf{p}$
*[2 marks available — 1 mark for correct $\overrightarrow{AB}$,
1 mark for correct $\overrightarrow{NA}$]*

Page 49 — Vectors

Q1 a) $\mathbf{u} = \begin{pmatrix} 2 \\ 3 \end{pmatrix}$, $\mathbf{v} = \begin{pmatrix} 5 \\ -3 \end{pmatrix}$

[2 marks available — 1 mark for $\mathbf{u}$, 1 mark for $\mathbf{v}$]

b) $\frac{1}{2}\mathbf{u} - 2\mathbf{v} = \begin{pmatrix} 1 \\ 1.5 \end{pmatrix} - \begin{pmatrix} 10 \\ -6 \end{pmatrix} = \begin{pmatrix} -9 \\ 7.5 \end{pmatrix}$

$\left|\frac{1}{2}\mathbf{u} - 2\mathbf{v}\right| = \left|\begin{pmatrix} -9 \\ 7.5 \end{pmatrix}\right| = \sqrt{(-9)^2 + 7.5^2}$
$= 11.72$ (2 d.p.)

*[3 marks available — 1 mark for correct resultant
vector, 1 mark for using Pythagoras' theorem,
1 mark for correct answer]*

Pages 50-51 – Revision Questions

Q1 Angles in any triangle add up to 180°.
Angles in any quadrilateral add up to 360°.

Q2 60°

Q3 A rhombus has four equal sides, two pairs of
parallel sides and two pairs of equal angles.
A kite has two pairs of equal sides and
one pair of equal angles.

Q4 Vertically opposite, alternate, allied (or interior)
and corresponding

Q5 a) First find missing angle in the triangle:
$180° - 83° - 71° = 26°$
Angles on a straight line add up to 180°:
$x = 180° - 26° = 154°$

b) Use corresponding angles: $y = 112°$

c) Use alternate angles and the fact that this is an
isosceles triangle: $z = 58°$

Q6 Exterior angle $= 360° \div 8 = 45°$

Q7 Sum of interior angles $= (9 - 2) \times 180° = 1260°$

Q8 1) A tangent and a radius meet at 90°.
2) Two radii form an isosceles triangle.
3) The perpendicular bisector of a chord passes
through the centre of a circle.
4) The angle at the centre of a circle is twice the
angle at the circumference.
5) The angle in a semicircle is 90°.
6) Angles in the same segment are equal.
7) Opposite angles in a cyclic quadrilateral are equal.
8) Tangents from the same point are the same length.

Q9 a) $x = 53°$ (angles in the same segment are equal)

b) $y = 90° - 21° = 69°$ (two radii form an isosceles
triangle, and a tangent and a radius meet at 90°)

c) First find the angle at the centre using the rule that
it is twice the angle at the circumference:
$57° \times 2 = 114°$
Then use the rule that two radii form an isosceles
triangle to find z: $z = (180° - 114°) \div 2 = 33°$

Q10 Quadrilateral A cannot be cyclic since opposite angles
must sum to 180° but $95° + 88° = 183° \neq 180°$.
On the other hand, the missing angle in Quadrilateral B
is $360° - 108° - 88° - 72° = 92°$. Then the sums
of opposite angles are $108° + 72° = 180°$ and
$88° + 92° = 180°$. So B is cyclic.

Q11 The angles are all the same.
The sides are all proportional.
Any two sides are proportional and the angle between
them is the same.

Q12 Work out the scale factor from the pair of
corresponding sides: $9 \div 3 = 3$.
Now use the scale factor to work out the required side
length: $x = 7.5 \div 3 = 2.5$ cm

Q13 Circumference $= \pi \times$ diameter $= 16\pi$ cm
Area $= \pi \times$ radius$^2 = \pi \times 8^2 = 64\pi$ cm^2
Since the question asked for exact values, you need to leave
your answer in terms of π.

Q14 Area of sector $= \frac{45}{360} \times \pi \times 10^2 = 39.27$ cm^2 (2 d.p.)

Q15 Let r be the radius of the sector and x the angle.
Perimeter $= 10 = r + r + 4 \Rightarrow r = 3$ cm
Arc length $= 4 = \frac{x}{360} \times 2 \times \pi \times 3 \Rightarrow 4 = \frac{\pi}{60}x$
$\Rightarrow x = \frac{4 \times 60}{\pi} = 76.4°$ (1 d.p.)

Answers

Q16 A regular hexagon can be divided into 6 equilateral triangles of side length 6 cm. To find the area of one of these triangles, use Pythagoras' Theorem to find the height:

Height = $\sqrt{6^2 - 3^2} = \sqrt{36 - 9} = \sqrt{27} = 3\sqrt{3}$ cm
Area of triangle = $0.5 \times 6 \times 3\sqrt{3} = 3 \times 3\sqrt{3} = 9\sqrt{3}$ cm^2
Area of hexagon = $6 \times 9\sqrt{3} = 54\sqrt{3}$ cm^2
Volume of prism = $54\sqrt{3} \times 11 = 594\sqrt{3}$
$\qquad\qquad\qquad = 1028.838...$
$\qquad\qquad\qquad = 1030$ cm^3 (3 s.f.)

Q17 a) Volume of cylinder = $\pi r^2 h = \pi \times 3^2 \times 8 = 72\pi$ cm^3
Volume of hemisphere = $\frac{2}{3}\pi r^3 = \frac{2}{3}\pi \times 3^3$
$\qquad\qquad\qquad\qquad = 18\pi$ cm^3
Total volume = $72\pi + 18\pi = 90\pi$ cm^3

b) Volume of cylinder = $\pi r^2 h = \pi \times 2^2 \times 9 = 36\pi$ cm^3
Volume of cone = $\frac{1}{3}\pi r^2 h = \frac{1}{3}\pi \times 2^2 \times 3 = 4\pi$ cm^3
Total volume = $36\pi + 4\pi = 40\pi$ cm^3

Q18 $5 \times 4^2 = 80$ cm^2
A scale factor of 4 makes the sides of a shape 4 times as long, but the area 16 times as big.

Q19 $a^2 + b^2 = c^2$
You use Pythagoras' theorem to find the missing side of a right-angled triangle.

Q20 $(\text{Length})^2 = 4^2 + 2.5^2$
Length $= \sqrt{16 + 6.25} = \sqrt{22.25} = 4.72$ m (3 s.f.)

Q21

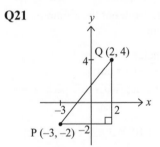

Length of horizontal side = $2 - (-3) = 5$
Length of vertical side = $4 - (-2) = 6$
$PQ^2 = 5^2 + 6^2$
$PQ = \sqrt{25 + 36} = \sqrt{61} = 7.8$ (1 d.p.)

Q22 $a^2 + b^2 + c^2 = d^2$

Q23 $d^2 = 5^2 + 6^2 + 9^2$
$d = \sqrt{25 + 36 + 81} = \sqrt{142} = 11.9$ m (3 s.f.)

Q24 a) P has x-coordinate 0 and the same y- and z-coordinates as the given point. So the coordinates are (0, 10, 3).

b) P has the same x-coordinate as the given point. In the y-direction, the smaller cuboid is half the length of the larger cube. Since the cube has a length of 4, P has y-coordinate 2. Finally, P is on the top of the cube, which has a height of 4, so the z-coordinate is 4. So the coordinates are (3, 2, 4).

Q25 Volume of cone = $4\pi = \frac{1}{3}\pi r^2 h$
$\Rightarrow 4\pi = \frac{1}{3}\pi \times 2^2 \times h \Rightarrow 4 = \frac{4}{3}h \Rightarrow h = \frac{4 \times 3}{4} = 3$
This is the z-coordinate of the base.
The full coordinates of the centre are (0, 0, 3).

Q26 a) $\overrightarrow{UV} = \overrightarrow{UX} + \overrightarrow{XV} = -\mathbf{u} + \mathbf{v} = \mathbf{v} - \mathbf{u}$

b) $\overrightarrow{WV} = \overrightarrow{WX} + \overrightarrow{XV} = \mathbf{u} + \mathbf{v}$

Q27 Multiplying by a scalar changes the size of a vector but not its direction (unless the scalar is negative).

Q28 a) (i) $\mathbf{a} - \mathbf{b} = \begin{pmatrix} 4 \\ -2 \end{pmatrix} - \begin{pmatrix} 7 \\ 6 \end{pmatrix} = \begin{pmatrix} 4 - 7 \\ -2 - 6 \end{pmatrix} = \begin{pmatrix} -3 \\ -8 \end{pmatrix}$

(ii) $5\mathbf{a} = 5 \times \begin{pmatrix} 4 \\ -2 \end{pmatrix} = \begin{pmatrix} 20 \\ -10 \end{pmatrix}$

(iii) $3\mathbf{a} + \mathbf{b} = 3 \times \begin{pmatrix} 4 \\ -2 \end{pmatrix} + \begin{pmatrix} 7 \\ 6 \end{pmatrix} = \begin{pmatrix} 12 + 7 \\ -6 + 6 \end{pmatrix} = \begin{pmatrix} 19 \\ 0 \end{pmatrix}$

(iv) $-4\mathbf{a} - 2\mathbf{b} = -4 \times \begin{pmatrix} 4 \\ -2 \end{pmatrix} - 2 \times \begin{pmatrix} 7 \\ 6 \end{pmatrix}$
$\qquad = \begin{pmatrix} -16 - 14 \\ 8 - 12 \end{pmatrix} = \begin{pmatrix} -30 \\ -4 \end{pmatrix}$

b) (i) $|\mathbf{a}| = \left| \begin{pmatrix} 4 \\ -2 \end{pmatrix} \right| = \sqrt{4^2 + (-2)^2} = \sqrt{20} = 2\sqrt{5}$

(ii) $|\mathbf{b}| = \left| \begin{pmatrix} 7 \\ 6 \end{pmatrix} \right| = \sqrt{7^2 + 6^2} = \sqrt{85}$

(iii) $|\mathbf{a} - \mathbf{b}| = \left| \begin{pmatrix} -3 \\ -8 \end{pmatrix} \right| = \sqrt{(-3)^2 + (-8)^2} = \sqrt{73}$

Q29 $\frac{1}{2}|\mathbf{p}| = \frac{1}{2}\sqrt{4^2 + 2^2 + (-2)^2} = \frac{1}{2}\sqrt{24} = \frac{1}{2} \times 2\sqrt{6} = \sqrt{6}$
$\left| \frac{1}{2}\mathbf{p} \right| = \sqrt{\left(\frac{4}{2}\right)^2 + \left(\frac{2}{2}\right)^2 + \left(\frac{-2}{2}\right)^2} = \sqrt{2^2 + 1^2 + (-1)^2}$
$\qquad\qquad\qquad = \sqrt{6}$

It actually turns out that $k|\mathbf{u}| = |k\mathbf{u}|$ for any scalar k and any vector $\mathbf{u}$. Cool, I guess...

Answers

Section Four — Trigonometric Skills

Page 52 —Trigonometric Graphs

Q1 a)

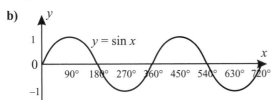

[2 marks available — 1 mark for correct shape and range, 1 mark for correct amplitude and period]

b)

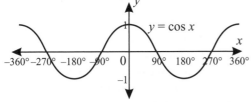

[2 marks available — 1 mark for correct shape and range, 1 mark for correct amplitude and period]

Page 53 — Trigonometric Graphs

Q1 a)

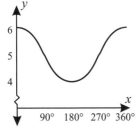

[2 marks available — 1 mark for correct shape including amplitude and period, 1 mark for correct translation 5 units in the positive y-direction]

b)

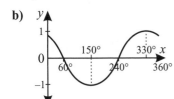

[2 marks available — 1 mark for correct shape including amplitude and period, 1 mark for correct translation 120° in the negative x-direction]

c)

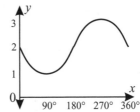

[3 marks available — 1 mark for correct shape including amplitude and period, 1 mark for translation 2 units in the positive y-direction, 1 mark for translation 180° in the positive x-direction]

Q2 A translation by a phase angle of 200° is the transformation $y = f(x - 200°)$. So this is a translation 200° in the positive x-direction. The point $x = 90°$ moves to $x = 90° + 200° = 290°$.

The sin graph has a peak at $x = 90°$ so the original y-coordinate of A is $y = 1$. The y-coordinate is unaffected by the translation so the y-coordinate after the translation is still 1.

So the coordinates are (290°, 1).

[2 marks available — 1 mark for correct x-coordinate, 1 mark for correct y-coordinate]

Page 54 — Trigonometric Graphs

Q1

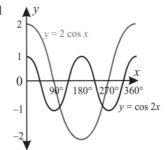

[4 marks available — 1 mark correct shape of $y = 2 \cos x$, 1 mark for correct amplitude of $y = 2 \cos x$, 1 mark correct shape of $y = \cos 2x$, 1 mark for correct period of $y = \cos 2x$,]

Q2 The maximum and minimum values of the transformed graph are 5 and –5, so $p = 5$.

The maximum value occurs 6 times, so $q = 6$.

[2 marks available — 1 mark for correct value of p, 1 mark for correct value of q]

Answers

Page 55 — Trigonometry — Sin, Cos, Tan

Q1 The ladder, floor and wall make a right-angled triangle as shown below. You need to find the length H.

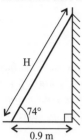

You know the length of the adjacent side and want the hypotenuse so using CAH from SOH CAH TOA:

$$\cos 74° = \frac{0.9}{H} \implies H = \frac{0.9}{\cos 74°} = 3.27 \text{ m (3 s.f.)}$$

[2 marks available — 1 mark for setting up equation using CAH, 1 mark for correct answer]

Page 56 — Related Angles

Q1 $\tan x = 0.3 \implies x = \tan^{-1}(0.3) = 16.7°$ (1 d.p.)
Using the graph of $y = \tan x$ and the fact that it repeats every 180°, the second solution is $180° + x = 196.7°$ (1 d.p.)

[2 marks available — 1 mark for each correct solution]

You could just as easily have used the T quadrant in the CAST diagram to get the same answer.

Q2 $\cos x = -\frac{1}{4} \implies x = \cos^{-1}\left(-\frac{1}{4}\right) = 104.5°$ (1 d.p.)
Using the C quadrant in the CAST diagram, the other solution is $360° - x = 255.5°$ (1 d.p.)

[2 marks available — 1 mark for each correct solution]

You could also have used the graph of $y = \cos x$ and seen that the distance between x and the y-axis is the same as the distance between the other solution and $y = 360°$.

Q3 $\sin x = -0.5 \implies x = \sin^{-1}(-0.5) = -30°$.
Since x is negative, use the C and T quadrants in the CAST diagram.
The T quadrant gives $180° + 30° = 210°$
and the C quadrant gives $360° - 30° = 330°$.

[2 marks available — 1 mark for each correct solution]

Page 57 — Solving Trig Equations

Q1
$$20 \sin x + 3 = 10$$
$$20 \sin x = 7$$
$$\sin x = \frac{7}{20}$$
$$x = \sin^{-1}\left(\frac{7}{20}\right) = 20.5° \text{ (1 d.p.)}$$

Using the graph of $y = \sin x$ or the CAST diagram, the other solution is $180° - x = 159.5°$ (1 d.p.)

[3 marks available — 1 mark for rearranging equation to make sin x the subject, 1 mark for first correct solution, 1 mark for second correct solution]

Page 58 — Trig Identities

Q1 $7 \tan x \cos x = 7 \dfrac{\sin x}{\cos x} \cos x = 7 \sin x$
so the equation is $7 \sin x = 5$
$$\sin x = \frac{5}{7}$$
$$x = \sin^{-1}\left(\frac{5}{7}\right) = 45.6° \text{ (1 d.p.)}$$

Using the graph of $y = \sin x$ or the CAST diagram, the other solution is $180° - x = 134.4°$ (1 d.p.).

[3 marks available — 1 mark for correct use of tan x identity, 1 mark for first correct solution, 1 mark for second correct solution]

Q2 $\cos^2 x \tan^2 x + \cos^2 x = \cos^2 x \dfrac{\sin^2 x}{\cos^2 x} + \cos^2 x$ *[1 mark]*
$$= \sin^2 x + \cos^2 x = 1 \text{ [1 mark]}$$

[2 marks available — 1 mark for replacing tan² x with sin² x/cos² x, 1 mark for fully simplified answer]

Q3 RHS $= \dfrac{\sin^2 x}{1 - \cos x} = \dfrac{1 - \cos^2 x}{1 - \cos x} = \dfrac{(1 + \cos x)(1 - \cos x)}{1 - \cos x}$
$$= 1 + \cos x = \text{LHS}$$

[3 marks available — 1 mark for using correct identity, 1 mark for using difference of two squares, 1 mark for simplifying]

Q4 $\dfrac{3 \sin^2 x \tan x}{\cos^2 x} = 3 \tan^2 x \tan x = 3 \tan^3 x$

[2 marks available — 1 mark for using tan identity, 1 mark for fully simplified answer]

Page 59 — The Sine and Cosine Rules

Q1 Area $= \dfrac{1}{2} ab \sin C = \dfrac{1}{2} (FG)(FH) \sin (GFH)$
$$= \frac{1}{2} \times 9 \times 12 \times \sin 37°$$
$$= 32.5 \text{ cm (3 s.f.)}$$

[2 marks available — 1 mark for using formula, 1 mark for correct answer]

Page 60 — The Sine and Cosine Rules

Q1 Using the sine rule:

$$\frac{24}{\sin 46°} = \frac{AB}{\sin 38°} \Rightarrow AB = \frac{24\sin 38°}{\sin 46°} = 20.5 \text{ cm (3 s.f.)}$$

[3 marks available — 1 mark for correct substitution into sine rule, 1 mark for rearranging for AB, 1 mark for correct value of AB]

Q2 Using the cosine rule:

$$\cos(RPQ) = \frac{9^2 + 15^2 - 13^2}{2 \times 9 \times 15} = \frac{137}{270}$$

$$RPQ = \cos^{-1}\left(\frac{137}{270}\right) = 59.5° \text{ (3 s.f.)}$$

[3 marks available — 1 mark for correct substitution into cosine rule, 1 mark for correct value of cos(RPQ), 1 mark for correct value of RPQ]

Page 61 — Trigonometry with Bearings

Q1 a) First use the information given to draw a diagram. Then use angle rules to find the other angles.

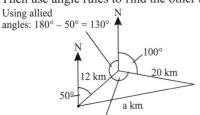

Cosine rule: $a^2 = b^2 + c^2 - 2bc \cos A$
$$= 12^2 + 20^2 - (2 \times 12 \times 20 \times \cos 130°)$$
$$= 852.53...$$
So $a = \sqrt{852.53...} = 29.198... = 29.2 \text{ km (1 d.p.)}$

The question says "calculate", which is a whopping clue that you shouldn't try and measure the length.

[4 marks available — 1 mark for using allied angles to find 130°, 1 mark for using angles round a point to find 130°, 1 mark for using cosine rule, 1 mark for correct answer]

b) To find the bearing, you need to work out the angle x in the diagram below:

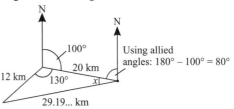

Using the cosine rule:
$$\cos x = \frac{20^2 + 29.198...^2 - 12^2}{2 \times 20 \times 29.198...} = 0.94...$$
$$x = \cos^{-1}(0.94...) = 18.35...°$$
Then the bearing is $360° - 80° - 18.35...°$
$$= 261.64...° = 262°.$$

[3 marks available — 1 mark for correct substitution into appropriate rule, 1 mark for correct value of x, 1 mark for correct answer]

Page 62 — Revision Questions

Q1

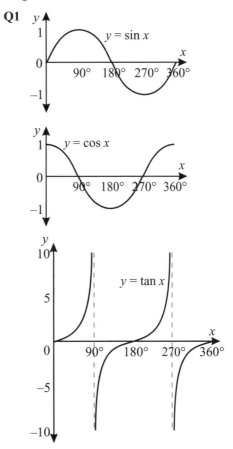

Answers

Q2 Period = 360°, Amplitude = 1

Q3 a)

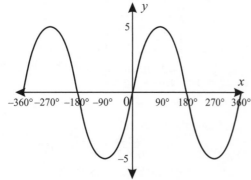

b)

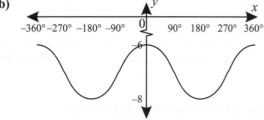

c)

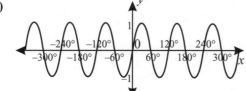

d)

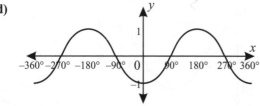

Q4 A phase angle of 60° means translating in the positive x-direction by 60°, i.e. the transformation f(x – 60°).

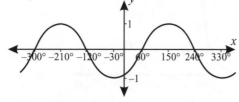

Q5 $\sin x = \dfrac{\text{opposite}}{\text{hypotenuse}}$

$\cos x = \dfrac{\text{adjacent}}{\text{hypotenuse}}$

$\tan x = \dfrac{\text{opposite}}{\text{adjacent}}$

Q6 $\cos x = \dfrac{7.6}{9.1} \Rightarrow x = \cos^{-1}\left(\dfrac{7.6}{9.1}\right) = 33.4°$ (1 d.p.)

Q7 $\tan 30° = \dfrac{XZ}{12} \Rightarrow XZ = 12 \tan 30° = 6.93$ cm (3 s.f.)

Q8 $\cos x = 0.9 \Rightarrow x = \cos^{-1}(0.9) = 25.8°$ (1 d.p.)
The other solution is $360° - x = 334.2°$ (1 d.p.)

Q9 $\sin x = -\dfrac{2}{3} \Rightarrow x = \sin^{-1}\left(-\dfrac{2}{3}\right) = -41.8103...°$
This is negative so use the T and C quadrants in the CAST diagram with 41.8103...°:
One solution is $180° + 41.8103...° = 221.8°$ (1 d.p.)
The other is $360° - 41.8103...° = 318.2°$ (1 d.p.)

Q10 Think about the graph of $\sin x$ — $\sin x$ is positive for $0° < x < 180°$, so $\sin 50° > 0$. $\sin x$ is negative for $180° < x < 360°$, so $\sin 270° < 0$ and $\sin 315° < 0$. $\sin x$ takes its minimum value at 270° ($\sin 270° = -1$). So the order is $\sin 270°$, $\sin 315°$, $\sin 50°$.

Q11 $3 \tan x - 3 = 5$
$3 \tan x = 8$
$\tan x = \dfrac{8}{3}$
$x = \tan^{-1}\left(\dfrac{8}{3}\right) = 69.4°$ (1 d.p.)
The other solution is $180° + x = 249.4°$ (1 d.p.)

Q12 Solve the equation $5 \sin x + 2 = 0$ to find the points where the graph intersects the x-axis.
$5 \sin x + 2 = 0$
$\sin x = -\dfrac{2}{5}$
$x = \sin^{-1}\left(-\dfrac{2}{5}\right) = -23.6°$ (1 d.p.)
But this negative value isn't in the right range.
Use the C and T quadrants in the CAST diagram with 23.6° since x is negative:
One solution is $180° + 23.6° = 203.6°$ (1 d.p.)
The other is $360° - 23.6° = 336.4°$ (1 d.p.)

Q13 $\tan x = \dfrac{\sin x}{\cos x}$

Q14 $\cos^2 x = 1 - \sin^2 x$

Q15 LHS $= 1 + \tan^2 x = \dfrac{\cos^2 x}{\cos^2 x} + \dfrac{\sin^2 x}{\cos^2 x} = \dfrac{\cos^2 x + \sin^2 x}{\cos^2 x}$
$= \dfrac{1}{\cos^2 x} = $ RHS

Q16 $\dfrac{\sin^4 x + \sin^2 x \cos^2 x}{-\sin^2 x} = -(\sin^2 x + \cos^2 x) = -1 = $ RHS

Q17 $(\sin y + \cos y)^2 + (\cos y - \sin y)^2$
$= (\sin^2 y + 2 \sin y \cos y + \cos^2 y)$
$\quad + (\cos^2 y - 2 \sin y \cos y + \sin^2 y)$
$= 2 \sin^2 y + 2 \cos^2 y = 2(\sin^2 y + \cos^2 y) = 2(1) = 2$

Q18 Sine rule: $\dfrac{a}{\sin A} = \dfrac{b}{\sin B} = \dfrac{c}{\sin C}$
Cosine rule: $a^2 = b^2 + c^2 - 2bc \cos A$
Area of a triangle $= \dfrac{1}{2} ab \sin C$

Answers

Q19 Two angles and any side: Sine rule
Two sides and an angle not enclosed: Sine rule
Two sides and the angle enclosed: Cosine rule
Three sides and no angles: Cosine rule

Q20

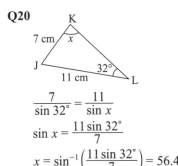

$$\frac{7}{\sin 32°} = \frac{11}{\sin x}$$

$$\sin x = \frac{11 \sin 32°}{7}$$

$$x = \sin^{-1}\left(\frac{11 \sin 32°}{7}\right) = 56.4° \text{ (3 s.f.)}$$

Q21

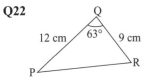

$$FG^2 = 8^2 + 9^2 - 2 \times 8 \times 9 \times \cos 47°$$
$$FG = \sqrt{64 + 81 - 144 \times \cos 47°} = 6.84 \text{ cm (3 s.f.)}$$

Q22

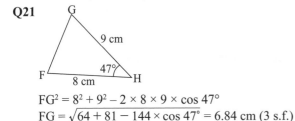

$$\text{Area} = \frac{1}{2} \times 12 \times 9 \times \sin 63° = 48.1 \text{ cm}^2 \text{ (3 s.f.)}$$

Q23 a) Angle WXZ = 180° − 112° − 46° = 22°

$$\frac{5.25}{\sin 22°} = \frac{XZ}{\sin 112°}$$

$$\frac{5.25}{\sin 22°} \times \sin 112° = XZ$$

XZ = 12.994... m
$$XY^2 = 12.994...^2 + 8.5^2$$
$$- 2 \times 12.994... \times 8.5 \times \cos 26°$$
$$= 42.55443...$$
XY = 6.52337... = 6.52 m (3 s.f.)

b) Area of XYZ = $\frac{1}{2} \times 12.994... \times 8.5 \times \sin 26°$
$$= 24.2092... \text{ m}^2$$

Area of WXZ = $\frac{1}{2} \times 12.994... \times 5.25 \times \sin 46°$
$$= 24.5365... \text{ m}^2$$
24.2092... + 24.5365... = 48.7457... m²
$$= 48.7 \text{ m}^2 \text{ (3 s.f.)}$$

Q24 a)

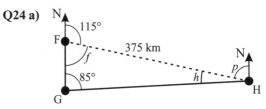

Using allied angles, angle p = 180° − 115° = 65°.
So the bearing is 360° − 65° = 295°.

b) Angle f = 180° − 115° = 65°.
Angle h = 180° − 85° − 65° = 30°.
Using the sine rule:

(i) $\frac{GF}{\sin h} = \frac{375}{\sin 85°} \Rightarrow GF = \frac{375 \sin 30°}{\sin 85°}$
$$= 188.2 \text{ km (1 d.p.)}$$

(ii) $\frac{GH}{\sin f} = \frac{375}{\sin 85°} \Rightarrow GH = \frac{375 \sin 65°}{\sin 85°}$
$$= 341.2 \text{ km (1 d.p.)}$$

Answers

Section Five — Statistical Skills

Page 63 — Mean, Median, Mode and Range

Q1 Mean $= \dfrac{1 + 3 + 14 + (-5) + 6 + \dots + 8}{15}$

$= \dfrac{79}{15} = 5.27$ (3 s.f.)

There are 15 values, so the median is the 8th value in the ordered list. In order, the values are:
$-14, -12, -5, -5, 0, 1, 3, \underline{6}, 7, 8, 10, 14, 18, 23, 25$
So median $= 6$
The mode is the most common value.
So mode $= -5$
Range = greatest value − least value
$= 25 - (-14) = 39$

[4 marks available — 1 mark for finding the mean, 1 mark for finding the median, 1 mark for finding the mode, 1 mark for finding the range]

Page 65 — Comparing Data Sets

Q1 a) In order the values are:
0.7, 1.1, 1.4, $\underline{1.6}$, 2.2, 2.6, 3.0
There are 7 values, so the median is the 4th value in the ordered list = 1.6 cm
Group the values either side of the median:
(0.7, 1.1, 1.4,) $\underline{1.6}$, (2.2, 2.6, 3.0)
The lower quartile is the middle value in the lower group = 1.1 cm and the upper quartile is the middle value in the upper group = 2.6 cm.
So the semi-interquartile range
$= \dfrac{2.6 - 1.1}{2} = 0.75$ cm

[3 marks available — 1 mark for finding the median, 1 mark for finding both quartiles, 1 mark for finding the semi-interquartile range]

b) The grubs in the second sample are longer, on average, since their median length is larger. There is more variation in the lengths of the grubs in the second sample, since the semi-interquartile range for the second sample is larger.

[2 marks available — 1 mark for a valid comment about the medians, 1 mark for a valid comment about the semi-interquartile ranges]

Page 67 — Scattergraphs

Q1 a) First find the gradient of the line:
$m = \dfrac{5 - 6.5}{8 - 3} = \dfrac{-1.5}{5} = -0.3$
Then substitute $m = -0.3$ and $(a, b) = (8, 5)$ into
$S - b = m(L - a)$
$S - 5 = -0.3(L - 8)$
$S - 5 = -0.3L + 2.4$
$S = -0.3L + 7.4$

[3 marks available — 1 mark for finding the gradient, 1 mark for a correct method to find the equation of a line, 1 mark for correct equation]

b) Substitute $L = 4$ into $S = -0.3L + 7.4$
$S = -0.3 \times 4 + 7.4$
$S = 6.2$ mph *[1 mark]*

Page 68 — Revision Questions

Q1 The <u>mode</u> is the most common value.
The <u>median</u> is the middle value when the data has been arranged in order of size.
The <u>mean</u> is the total of the data divided by the number of data values.
The <u>range</u> is the difference between the highest and lowest data values.

Q2 Mode $= 31$
There are 11 values, so the median is the 6th value in the ordered list: 2, 8, 11, 15, 22, $\underline{24}$, 27, 30, 31, 31, 41
So median $= 24$
Mean $= \dfrac{2 + 8 + 11 + 15 + 22 + \dots + 41}{11} = \dfrac{242}{11} = 22$
Range $= 41 - 2 = 39$

Q3 a) In order the values are:
55, 62, 74, $\underline{85, 98}$, 100, 112, 132
There are 8 values, so the median is halfway between the 4th and 5th values.
So the median is $\dfrac{85 + 98}{2} = \dfrac{183}{2} = 91.5$ p/kg

b) Mean $= \dfrac{62 + 100 + 74 + 112 + 85 + \dots + 98}{8}$
$= \dfrac{718}{8} = 89.75$ p/kg

Answers

Q4 a) In order the values are:
18, 27, <u>35</u>, 47, 62
There are 5 values, so the median is the 3rd value = 35.
Group the values either side of the median:
(18, 27,) <u>35</u>, (47, 62)
The lower quartile is halfway between the 1st and 2nd values.
So the lower quartile is $\dfrac{18 + 27}{2} = \dfrac{45}{2} = 22.5$.
The upper quartile is halfway between the 4th and 5th values.
So the upper quartile is $\dfrac{47 + 62}{2} = \dfrac{109}{2} = 54.5$.

b) Interquartile range = $Q_3 - Q_1$ = 54.5 − 22.5 = 32

c) Semi-interquartile range = IQR ÷ 2 = 32 ÷ 2 = 16

Q5 List the values in order and split into equal groups:
(67, 68, <u>68</u>, 70, 71,) (72, 72, <u>73</u>, 74, 75)
The lower quartile is the middle value in the lower group = 68, and the upper quartile is the middle value in the upper group = 73.
So the semi-interquartile range = $\dfrac{73 - 68}{2} = 2.5$.

Q6 First find the mean: $\bar{x} = \dfrac{3 + 8 + 10}{3} = \dfrac{21}{3} = 7$
Then find $(x - \bar{x})^2$ for each value:

x	$(x - \bar{x})$	$(x - \bar{x})^2$
3	−4	16
8	1	1
10	3	9
	Total	26

Now substitute into the standard deviation formula:
$$s = \sqrt{\frac{\sum(x - \bar{x})^2}{n - 1}} = \sqrt{\frac{26}{3 - 1}} = \sqrt{13}$$
So b = 13.
You can use the alternative version of the formula if you find it easier.

Q7 First find the mean:
$$\bar{x} = \frac{2 + 3 + 3 + 3 + 4 + \ldots + 10}{10} = \frac{50}{10} = 5$$
Then find $(x - \bar{x})^2$ for each value:

x	$(x - \bar{x})$	$(x - \bar{x})^2$
2	−3	9
3	−2	4
3	−2	4
3	−2	4
4	−1	1
5	0	0
5	0	0
7	2	4
8	3	9
10	5	25
	Total	60

Now substitute into the standard deviation formula:
$$s = \sqrt{\frac{\sum(x - \bar{x})^2}{n - 1}} = \sqrt{\frac{60}{10 - 1}}$$
$$= \frac{\sqrt{60}}{\sqrt{9}} = \frac{\sqrt{4}\sqrt{15}}{3} = \frac{2\sqrt{15}}{3}$$
So c = 2 and d = 15.
To get the standard deviation into its simplest form, you need to simplify the surd on the top of the fraction (see p.11).

Q8 a) Mean = $\bar{x} = \dfrac{18 + 25 + 32 + 21 + 29}{5}$
$$= \frac{125}{5} = 25$$
Find $(x - \bar{x})^2$ for each value:

x	$(x - \bar{x})$	$(x - \bar{x})^2$
18	−7	49
25	0	0
21	−4	16
32	7	49
29	4	16
	Total	130

Substitute into the standard deviation formula:
$$s = \sqrt{\frac{\sum(x - \bar{x})^2}{n - 1}} = \sqrt{\frac{130}{5 - 1}} = \sqrt{32.5}$$
$$= 5.70\ldots = 5.7 \text{ (1 d.p.)}$$

b) Saleem dealt with more queries each day, on average, since his mean number of queries was higher. There was less variation in the number of queries per day Jeff dealt with, since his standard deviation was smaller.

Answers

Q9 a) Summer semi-interquartile range
$= \frac{33 - 20}{2} = 6.5$ mins

Winter semi-interquartile range
$= \frac{40 - 19}{2} = 10.5$ mins

b) It took Henry longer to get to work in the summer, on average, since the summer median time is higher. The summer journey times are more consistent, since the semi-interquartile range is smaller.

Q10 a) E.g.

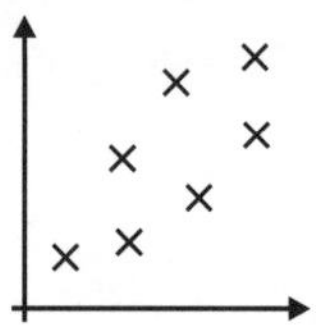

b) E.g.

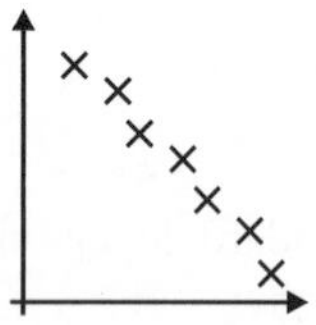

c) E.g.

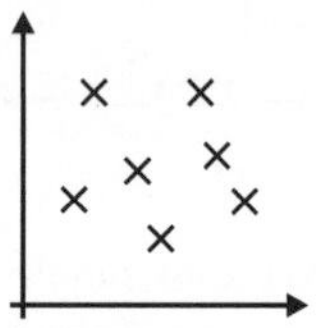

Q11 First find the gradient of the line:
$m = \frac{60 - 15}{70 - 20} = \frac{45}{50} = 0.9$

Then substitute $m = 0.9$ and $(a, b) = (20, 15)$ into
$P - b = m(M - a)$
$P - 15 = 0.9(M - 20)$
$P - 15 = 0.9M - 18$
$P = 0.9M - 3$

Q12 Substitute $M = 40$ into $P = 0.9M - 3$:
$P = 0.9 \times 40 - 3$
$P = 33$

Section Six — Reasoning Skills

Page 70 — Reasoning Skills — Worked Example

Q1 As the vertices of the octagon touch the circumference of the circle, you can make a triangle formed by two radii and one side of the octagon as shown (the angle between the radii is $360° \div 8 = 45°$, as you could form 8 of these triangles):

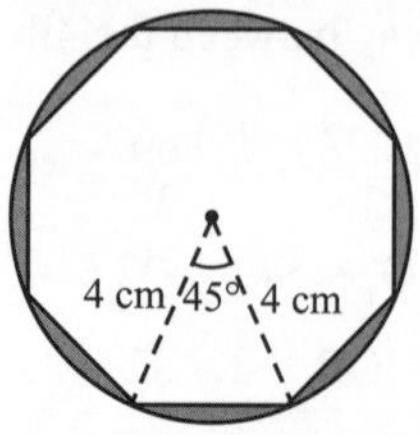

The area of this triangle is:
$\frac{1}{2}ab \sin C = \frac{1}{2} \times 4 \times 4 \times \sin 45° = 5.656...$
So the area of the octagon is $8 \times 5.656... = 45.254...$
The area of the circle is: $\pi r^2 = \pi \times 4^2 = 50.265...$
So the shaded area is: $50.265... - 45.254... = 5.010...$
$= 5.0$ cm^2 (2 s.f.)

[5 marks available — 1 mark for dividing the octagon up into triangles with the correct angle, 1 mark for a correct method to find the area of one triangle, 1 mark for the correct area of the octagon, 1 mark for finding the area of the circle, 1 mark for the correct final answer to the specified degree of accuracy]

Index

Formula Sheet

There's a lot to learn for your National 5 maths exam — that's no lie. Thankfully, you'll get some formulas given to you at the start of your paper. These ones, to be precise...

The roots of $ax^2 + bx + c = 0$ are $x = \dfrac{-b \pm \sqrt{(b^2 - 4ac)}}{2a}$

Sine rule: $\dfrac{a}{\sin A} = \dfrac{b}{\sin B} = \dfrac{c}{\sin C}$

Cosine rule: $a^2 = b^2 + c^2 - 2bc \cos A$ or $\cos A = \dfrac{b^2 + c^2 - a^2}{2bc}$

Area of a triangle: $A = \dfrac{1}{2} ab \sin C$

Volume of a sphere: $V = \dfrac{4}{3} \pi r^3$

Volume of a cone: $V = \dfrac{1}{3} \pi r^2 h$

Volume of a pyramid: $V = \dfrac{1}{3} Ah$

Standard deviation: $s = \sqrt{\dfrac{\sum(x - \bar{x})^2}{n - 1}}$ or $s = \sqrt{\dfrac{\sum x^2 - \dfrac{(\sum x)^2}{n}}{n - 1}}$

(where n is the sample size)